TALK WITH YOUR KIDS: BIG IDEAS

Conversations about democracy, infinity, environment, war and punishment, humanity and 77 other big ideas

MICHAEL PARKER

Talk With Your Kids: Big Ideas
Conversations about democracy, infinity, environment, war and punishment,
humanity and 77 other big ideas

Written by Michael Parker

First published in 2014 by Jane Curry Publishing

PO Box 780, Edgecliff NSW 2027
AUstralia

www.janecurrypublishing.com
www.janecurrypublishing.com.au

National Library of Australia cataloguing-in-publication data:

Author: Michael Parker
Title: *Talk With Your Kids: Big Ideas*
Conversations about democracy, infinity environment, war and punishment,
humanity and 77 other big ideas

ISBN 978-1-922190-89-5 (Print edition)
ISBN 978-0-9924532-1-3 (Epub Edition)
ISBN 978-1-922190-20-8 (Epdf/Mobi Edition)

Cover and internal design by Deborah Parry
Editorial: Sarah Plant
Production: Jasmine Standfield
Printed by McPhersons Printing Australia

CONTENTS

Introduction for Parents

Probably one of the greatest things about your very young children was their boundless curiosity. Everything in the world around them was wonderful and shiny and new; be it a toy, a new room, an un-walked path, or that disgusting, half chewed thing your dog brought in from the garden.

However, as they get older somehow that curiosity starts to close down a little in many kids. They are still interested and open, but that insatiable desire to know more and more about the world lessens.

This book is about keeping the door of curiosity open. And it is about more. It is about taking the door off the frame and knocking down the wall to reveal the amazing vista of wonderful, important, confronting, energising ideas, ready for the thinking.

For as they get older, kids get better at thinking. They know more, they will be more abstract and they can handle bigger and bigger concepts. So it is wonderful to show them ideas to keep that curiosity churning along. Schools at their best do it. But why should they have all the fun? If you have to supervise the homework and make the school lunches, at least you could also be talking with them about cloning, memories, capitalism and the meaning of life. I have aimed most of the conversations here at younger teenagers, but I also think you could have some of the discussions when they are nine, and many of them when they are ninety (if you live that long).

I think it is also important that your kids come across many of these ideas before they are fully fledged adults because the ideas are important in and of themselves. Kids think all of the time- so they should spend some time talking about what thoughts *are*. They live in a capitalist system every day — so at least they should talk about what capitalism *is* (just like a fish should probably talk about the water). One day you and they will both die — so they should talk about dying sometime too. Admittedly they will probably never turn into a bat, but it is great fun to talk about what would happen if they did. All of this is part of living an examined life.

As well, I hope that that the conversations will help you and your kids get on with each other. The conversations may mean that there is open, thoughtful, substantial discussions happening with your kids during those years that they otherwise might retreat into a teenage shell. It may mean you get to talk with your kids about things other than scheduling, homework and why their room is still a mess. (Part of this can be selfish. Wouldn't it be great when they are giving your eulogy for them to say; '*And we used to have the most FANTASTIC conversations about stuff that mattered*') They might see you as a place to go when the big questions need to be asked. And you might fully see them as amazing, developing young people with great ideas of their own.

SO HOW TO GET YOUR KIDS INTERESTED IN TALKING BIG IDEAS

Some of these ideas will work with your family, others won't.

- You can have a copy in the car glovebox to get conversations started on drives.

- Have a regular 'event' pizza dinner with conversations about big ideas. Unfortunately you may have to forsake a healthy evening meal in order to have the conversation (of course, if you feel you can get lentil soup and Big Ideas into the same sitting, go for your life).

- You can create an expectation of 'chatting about a big idea' at any regular time- bath time for younger kids, after dinner or before bed for older kids.

- You can leave the book lying around for your kids to flick through. They may well find some ideas that interest them.

- Use the book as a goad to look for big ideas as your kids get on with their lives. Perhaps a family or schoolyard event/ crisis will prompt a big discussion. Perhaps you can catch issues as they come up in the news. Sometimes you can lever off the homework they are doing into more interesting areas. You can also use net resources to get conversations going.

HOW TO TALK WITH YOUR KIDS ABOUT BIG IDEAS

I have written more about how to talk 'Big Ideas' in the book 'Talk With Your Kids: Ethics', but some of the points warrant repeating.

- Don't feel the need to work, question by question, through the book. Choose any topic you like. Then choose any question you like.

- Similarly don't feel the need for the conversation to be a whole seminar's worth of big thinking. Sometimes five minutes is good. Sometimes forty five minutes is good. It depends on the rhythms of the family.

- Let your kids do as much of the actual talking as possible. Only talk as much as you need to in order to fan the flames of discussion. You may remember conversations with authority figures when you were a child. If they did most of the talking, you probably felt hectored and tuned out pretty quickly. So if you find that you are talking more than half the time, then something may well be going wrong.

- Don't provide them with the 'actual' answer to any of these questions. They will not feel valued if they feel you are letting them flail around before you unveil - voilà! - the true answer. It is about respecting their thoughts, their ideas and their creativity.

- It is your child's mental process that is the interesting thing, not yours. So sound like you are interested in what they say. You can do this using all of the conversational lubricant like 'that's interesting', or 'I hadn't thought of it like that' or 'tell me more about that'. Better still, really be interested in what they say, even if it is not profound or earthshattering. Then all of the encouragement will come naturally.

- Play devil's advocate. It is usually okay to argue the other side of an issue (topics such as Nazism excepted). Just make sure that your kids know that you are playing devil's advocate to keep the conversation going, and that you are not being contrary for the sake of it.

- Be a conversational traffic cop who keeps the ideas flowing. Keep tabs on the discussion. Say things such as 'how does this relate to what you were saying before?', 'have you got an example of that?', 'how is that different to what your sister just said?' etc.

Good luck. And have fun.

BIG IDEA 1:
Would you rather... ?

a) Would you rather:
   a. win five million dollars or
   b. win one million dollars and have 20 neighbours all win one million dollars as well?

b) Would you rather:
   a. be really rich but have no family or
   b. really poor but have a big loving family?

c) Would you rather:
   a. have half the world rich and half the world poor or
   b. everyone in the world semi-poor (or semi-rich)?

d) What are the most important things in life?

a) Would you rather:
   a. lose your sense of sight or
   b. lose your sense of hearing?

b) Would you rather:
   a. lose your sense of taste or

b. lose your sense of smell?

c) **Would you rather:**
  a. lose your sense of touch or
  b. lose your sense of hearing?

d) **Which of your senses are the most important to you, and why?**

a) **Would you rather:**
  a. go on an overseas trip or
  b. get a top of the line new television for your house?

b) **Would you rather:**
  a. take an overseas trip to a fabulous beach or
  b. take an overseas trip to a fabulous city?

c) **Would you rather:**
  a. travel through a Western country (eg Germany) or
  b. travel through an Asian country (eg Thailand)?

d) **Why do people travel? Is travel good for people, and why?**

a **Would you rather:**
  a. live in a country where the military ran everything and shot people or
  b. live in a country where the government had no control and there was a lot of crime?

b) **Would you rather:**
  a. lose your freedoms (eg to vote, to have free speech) or
  b. lose all your family's money?

c) **Would you rather:**
  a. protest about a military regime or

b. keep quiet and get on with your work?

d) What do you think about living in a country with freedoms and elections?

a) **Would you rather be:**
   a. the strongest person in your year or
   b. the smartest person in your year?

b) **Would you rather be:**
   a. the smartest person in your year or
   b. the most popular person in your year?

c) **Would you rather be:**
   a. the most popular person in your year or
   b. the richest person in your year?

d) **What matters most to you at school?**

EXTREMELY SERIOUS MATTERS INDEED...

a) **Would you rather be:**
   a. eaten by a shark or
   b. stung to death by bees?

b) **Would you rather eat:**
   a. an oyster sandwich or
   b. a broccoli milkshake?

c) **Would you rather:**
   a. have your eyes fall out or
   b. have your legs fall off?

d) **Would you rather be turned into:**

a. a rat or

b. a slug?

(Note: you can make up your own examples to gross out your brother/sister/parents)

a) **On TV would you rather watch:**

a. a movie or

b a game of sport?

b) **Would you rather go to:**

a. the theatre or

b. the movies?

c) **Would you rather go to:**

a. a concert by your favourite musician or

b. the grand final of your favourite team?

d) **What do you like watching the most?**

a) **Would you rather be:**

a. a fabulously wealthy and famous sports star or

b. incredibly rich with not much work to do?

b) **Would you rather:**

a. live until 65 with the most fabulous amazing life or

b. live until 95 with a pretty good life the whole time?

c) **What do you want most?**

BIG IDEA 2:
Are you in the middle of a dream?

BACKGROUND BRIEFING

Look around you. Everything seems normal — just like every other day. Perhaps things are a bit strange because you are reading an odd book about Big Ideas, but that's not so bad. But wait... is this *really* real? Are you actually even awake? Or maybe... just perhaps... you are *in the middle of a dream*, right now. A realistic dream, a slightly dull dream even... but a dream nonetheless.

You don't think so? You are convinced you are not in a dream right now? Well if you are so sure... go right ahead and *prove it*.

a. Dreams are often about real life and feel like real life — JUST LIKE NOW
b. Dreams often have something strange happen in them — JUST LIKE NOW
c. Sometimes in a dream you have a weird feeling that maybe you are actually in a dream — JUST LIKE NOW

> TIP:
> A way of doing this is
> to play a game where one person in
> the conversation tries to prove that
> they are not in a dream and the other
> person in the conversation argues
> that they CAN'T prove it.

Conversation

a) If this is the dream, try to wake up.

b) People often say that the way of proving something isn't a dream is to pinch yourself. Try it. Does this really prove that you are not in a dream?

c) Could the dream have started two minutes ago, and everything you remember about your past is just a part of the dream?

d) Could you be your parents, dreaming that you are your own children?

e) Could you actually be living in 1800AD and dreaming of an amazing future with motor cars, microwave ovens and computers?

f) If THIS is the dream, take other guesses at what could be your real life. Use your imagination.

g) If you can't prove that this is not a dream can you prove:
   a. that your school exists?
   b. that we are on planet earth?
   c. that you exist?

P.S.

Rene Descartes suggests that it is impossible to prove that we are not in the middle of a dream. He also suggests that an evil demon may have kidnapped us and connected our brain up to a box called 'The Experience Machine'. This box pumps experiences into our brain like a virtual reality programme, then we are fooled into thinking we were really experiencing things.

a) Can we prove that we are not hooked up to an experience machine or a computer?

b) Make up the story for a movie blockbuster which involves people being caught in dreams or machines that look like the real world.

BIG IDEA 3:
Simulated reality

BACKGROUND BRIEFING

At the moment computer games on screens and with goggles can make it feel like you are 'really there' — this is virtual reality. However, virtual reality in the future may go much, much further and become 'simulated reality'. It may mean connecting your brain to a computer and having lots of electrical data sent directly into your brain. These impulses will bypass your eyes, your nose and skin and go straight to your cerebral cortex. These impulses will make you *think* you are seeing, tasting and feeling, but you are not 'really'. You will be immersed in a whole world that feels real but is just a computer simulation.

Conversation

☞ 'SAM'S SIMULATION SHOP OPENS IN YOUR MALL... ALL THE FUN IN THE WORLD, CHEAP!!!'

Imagine that you go into this simulation shop. Sam welcomes you and shows you how it works. All you have to do is lie back on one of the comfortable seats and get connected to a computer. You then close your eyes and have all of the sense data pumped straight in your brain so you feel as if you are really *there*. Sam asks if you would like to have a go.

a) **Would you use Sam's shop:**

    a. to go on 'afternoon holidays' to the most exciting parts of the world and do exciting stuff like paragliding, mountain climbing etc?

    b. to play a 'game' in which you are an action hero in a thriller or a romantic hero?

    c. to take your family and go on a 'one week holiday' to an amazing beach resort or to see the highlights of Europe?

    d. to play a week long action game with your family as a holiday?

b) **If you went on a simulated reality one week beach holiday with your family, would you have 'really' gone on a beach holiday? Would your experiences be real ones? Would your memories be real ones? Would your emotions have been real ones?**

Sam has a brand new product he offers to you. When you are inside the simulation, you FORGET that you are inside a simulation. Instead, you think it is the real thing. He offers you a variety of five hour games.

a) **Would you have a go in a game in which:**

    a. you really think you are on the world's most exclusive beach having an amazing holiday?

b. you really think you are a Tom Cruise style action hero saving the world from mastermind criminals?

c. you really think you are Tom Cruise, living the life of a Hollywood superstar?

d. you really think you are the most popular, sporty, smartest person in your school having a fantastic day?
(Unless of course you already are, in which case you may already be in the simulation).

b) Would you enter a game in which you spent part of it thinking you may die? Even though you know before going in that you would be completely safe.

c) When you came out of this game, do you think you would suffer some sort of trauma (as if it really happened) or would it be more like a dream (where you get over it as soon as you wake up)?

The next time you go into Sam's shop it is looking darker and you can see long rows of people connected to computers behind the shopfront. Sam tells you he has an amazing new offer. For not much money you can be connected up to a computer for the rest of your life. You can do it on your own, or you can bring your whole family and be connected together. You can spend a day programming exactly the life you would want to live, then put on the headset and live it. You can pre-programme a life in which you are massively successful, popular, loved, confident and attractive. You can make yourself a superspy, a love god, a sports god or a ground-breaking genius (or all of these). You would never know you were living a simulation.

a) Do you take it? Why/why not? What is hard about the choice?

b) What if Sam offered a programme that went for five years instead of your whole life? Or he offered you a chance to live in all sorts of different times (as a King, a President, or an explorer in the future). Or he offered any other combination you could dream up?

c) Are these experiences real? Have you lived a life in a simulation or not?

P.S.

The philosopher Nick Bostrom came up with a startling idea. He said it may be possible for a future society to create virtual reality worlds on computers with programmed people inside them who THINK they are alive, but are just part of the simulation. If this happened, there wouldn't just be one programme, there would be hundreds of billions of programmes. Indeed, each time the programme was copied, new versions of the people would be created (just like when a singer makes a record, millions of copies of the record are created). If this were true, it would be much more likely that any one person is one of the billions of copies, rather than one of the originals. This also means that YOU are much more likely to be a computer simulation than a 'real' flesh and blood person.

Conversation

a) Have a conversation about Nick Bostrom's idea. What do you think of it? Is it likely that you are just a simulation? Do you see any problems with his idea?

b) Do you think computer programmes could ever create mini programmes who thought that they were people?

BIG IDEA 4:
Acts and Intentions in crime

BACKGROUND BRIEFING

For us to think that an act (such as bank robbery) is criminal it usually needs to have two elements — an intent (you intended to rob the bank) and an act (you actually robbed the bank). Intent is called 'mens rea' and the act is called 'actus reus' in courts. But what happens when there is only intent or only act?

Conversation

a) Imagine that Percy, Allan and Sue decide that they hate their local council and the only solution is to blow up the council chambers one night. Do you think that they have committed a terrorist crime when:

    a. they make plans on a blueprint to blow up the council chambers?

b. they purchase materials for a bomb on the internet?

c. they assemble the bomb?

d. they walk out of the house to plant a bomb but haven't got to the council chambers yet?

e. Imagine that Allan decides he can't go through with the bombing two streets away from the council chambers. He runs away from the others. Is he still guilty of helping commit the bombing?

b) Enrico has terrible waking nightmares in which he also walks in his sleep. One morning he wakes from a terrible nightmare in which he robbed a bank and shot a bank teller. He looks at the end of his bed and there is a bag full of money there. Then he turns on the television and sees stories of 'The Pyjama Robber' who has held up a bank and shot a bank teller. CCTV footage on the TV shows that it is clearly him. Is Enrico guilty of robbing the bank?

c) Peter is playing 'Cowboys and Indians' with his father's plastic toy gun. He shoots his friend Ngo and a sharp bang goes off. It turns out that the gun was real and Ngo is lying on the ground. Is Peter guilty of shooting Ngo?

P.S.

Pierre Laplace (1749–1827) was a determinist who thought that if you could take a complete physical picture of the world at one moment you could predict the events that would happen in the future.

More conversation

a) Imagine that police have invented 'The Laplace Machine' that can tell what is going to happen for a full day in the future. In particular it can tell who is going to commit crimes, including crimes that people didn't know that they were about to commit.

    a. Would it be okay to arrest for murder a man who was about to murder his business partner in a fit of rage, even if he had no idea that he was about to do it?

    b. Would it be okay to arrest for murder a woman who was going to murder her husband in an hour's time, even if she had made plans but didn't know if she was going to go through with it?

(Note: this is also the premise of the Phillip K Dick novella *Minority Report*.)

BIG IDEA 5:
Capitalism

BACKGROUND BRIEFING

Capitalism is where individual people or companies (not the government) own most of the shops, farms, businesses, banks etc in a country. The people try to sell things (eg apples, newspapers, movies) for more than it cost to make or buy them. If they do this they make a *profit*, most of which they get to keep. This is known as the free market.

Conversation

a) How could you make a profit if you had just:

   a. grown 1000 apples?

   b. made the new superman movie for $200 million dollars?

   c. invented a new car engine that ran on seawater?

What might be hard about making a profit?

b) Why do people work hard? Why do YOU work hard? Could it be to:

a. help other people?

b. make money for themselves?

c. stay interested in what they do?

d. make time to do something else (eg go watch theatre, play sport etc)?

c) Imagine that you have started up a company making sneakers and you get 50 people to come to work for you. How much should you pay them:

a. as little as possible, after all it's your company and they can always go somewhere else?

b. enough for them to have a good life (as long as the company makes enough money)?

c. a share of the profits for those who work just as hard as you?

Why?

d) Imagine that you own a company that can easily turn the water from Lake Bicarb into Coke. It only works on this one lake. However, the process makes an enormous amount of smoke. How much should you think about all of the following people when deciding how much Coke to make:

a. the people who gave you a lot of money to start up the company in the first place?

b. you and your family who will make a lot of money?

c. the people who live on the shore of Lake Bicarb?

d. all the people who will be breathing in the smoke?

e. the Coca Cola company, who invented Coke?

P.S.

In 1776, Adam Smith wrote 'The Wealth of Nations' which many people see as the Capitalist Bible. He wrote that if companies (eg companies selling apples) compete with each other, this will drive down prices and will be good for the consumer (eg the people who buy the apples). He also said that government should stay out of the market and let companies fight it out amongst themselves. He thought that the invisible hand of the market would mean that efficient companies would go well and bad companies would fail.

Other economists, such as Alan Marshall, criticised Adam Smith. Marshall said that men were just as important as money. He thought that we should pay a lot of attention to 'human welfare'. If humans are being trampled on by a company making money, then the company should be stopped (or at least slowed down).

Conversation

a) Imagine a country in which computer companies, publishers, supermarkets and car makers were allowed to do anything they want to compete with each other (except for criminal acts such as shooting employees or burning down factories). What do you think would happen to:

a. the quality of the cars, computers etc? (up or down)

b. the price of the computers, books etc? (up or down)

    c. the wages of the people employed by the companies?
      (more or less)

    d. the larger companies? (survive or die)

    e. the smaller companies? (survive or die)

b) If you were the government, would you want to put controls on what companies did? What controls would you introduce?

c) In an argument between Adam Smith and Alan Marshall, who do you think should win?

d) Imagine that a US mining company could only make profits if it also put workers in serious danger underground. Should the company:

    a. put the workers in serious danger?

    b. close down?

BIG IDEA 6:
Should we get involved in deposing tyrants?

BACKGROUND BRIEFING

There are a number of countries on Earth with leaders who routinely imprison, torture and kill those who oppose them. They may be using the country as a way of making themselves rich (a kleptocracy) or to enforce one very narrow way of life on everyone. Some dictators such as Kim Jong Un (North Korea) and Bashar Al Assad (Syria) are well known. However, there are many others.

Conversation

a) Should oppressed people in a country such as North Korea stand up and demand elections or should they keep their heads down so that they are not killed?

b) If your family was going to run a heartless tyrannical state with yourself as leader, what would you do with:

a. the army?
b. the education system?
c. your closest allies (who could also try to overthrow you)?
d. the media?
e. your family?

Does having a conversation about this help explain why more people do not rise up and overthrow a tyranny?

c) If we lived in a tyranny, would we want the army from somewhere else (eg Europe) to invade us and overthrow the dictator? Why/why not? What would be good about this and what would be the dangers?

d) Does a powerful country (eg the USA) have a moral duty to invade a country with a dictator and overthrow him/her? Does a powerful country have a moral duty NOT to get involved in the internal affairs of another country?

e) Would it make a difference if:
a. the invasion could occur with not many people dying?
b. the invasion could be done without huge expense?
c. as a bonus the country invaded has a lot of gold that could be mined?
d. many people in the country WANT a powerful nation to invade?
e. the new government coming in might well be as bad as the old one (but it might not)?

f) The United Nations is a body created 70 years ago that 'represents' all of the countries on Earth. They do not have a military force, although they do have some control of 'peacekeeping' forces that groups of nations provide. Could the United Nations itself raise a military force that could be used to overthrow tyrannies? Should it do this? What would be the dangers of the United Nations getting a military force of its own?

g) Talk about (or research) recent invasions of countries with dictatorships (eg Afghanistan, Iraq) and recent civil wars (eg Syria). What do the facts of these cases make you think about overthrowing dictators? Was it worth it? Would it be worth it?

BIG IDEA 7:
Getting really old

Age is a question of mind over matter. If you don't mind, it doesn't matter. (Leroy 'Satchel' Paige)

The years teach much which the days never knew. (Ralph Waldo Emerson)

You are as young as your faith, as old as your doubt; as young as your self-confidence, as old as your fear; as young as your hope, as old as your despair. (Douglas MacArthur)

A man is not old until regrets take the place of dreams. (John Barrymore)

Youth is a wonderful thing. What a crime to waste it on children. (George Bernard Shaw)

Conversation

a) Look at your grandparents, or some other older people. What might be better about their lives than yours? What might be better about your lives than theirs?

b) Look at your parents. What is better about their lives than yours? What is better about your lives than theirs?

c) Imagine that you could take a pill that gave you incredible good luck, good looks and good fortune until you were 35, but then you had to die at 36. Would you take it? Why/why not?

d) If you were told that you were going to die at the age of 80 years and one day old (unless you did something really silly like jump off a cliff) what would you want to have done in all of that time?

e) What gets better as you get older? What gets worse?

f) Should you look forward to getting old? Why? What is there to avoid?

g) What things do you think might be important to people as they get older?

h) Look at each of the quotes above. What do you think they mean? Do you agree with them? Is there any advice in there that you think is good?

i) When you get very old do you think you would be more or less afraid of dying?

BIG IDEA 8:
Do people start off good or bad?

a) Imagine that a Boeing 747 plane you are flying on crashes onto a paradise island and no-one is hurt. When you get out there are sparkling beaches, beautiful forests and plenty of healthy food for everyone (mainly fruit). It turns out the cargo hold of the plane had crates of seeds for wheat, rice and corn. However, all of the communication equipment is down and no-one is going to find you.

   a. Do you think that there will be a leader of the group in the first few days? Who? What sort of person will they probably be?

   b. What will people do for the first few weeks? (eg all get together and talk? Try to mark out their own territory?)

   c. Imagine that a crate of guns is found in the plane's cargo hold after a week. Will anything happen differently now?

   d. What do you think the paradise island will be like to live in:

      i.   after a month?

      ii. after a year?

      iii. after ten years?

b) If cavemen in Africa from tens of thousands of years ago had stayed in caves/the jungle, what would their lives be like now? How would they be better or worse than our own lives?

c) Do you think that people are kinder in large cities (where there are large groups of all sorts of different people) or in small towns (where everyone knows each other)?

d) What do you remember about kindergarten? What were the other children there like (ie compared to the people you know now?)

P.S.

Different philosophers have had their say about whether people are naturally good or bad. Jean Jacques Rosseau (1712–1778) held that people were at their best when they were in a 'state of nature' in small groups. He thought that they would be 'noble savages'. This was somewhere halfway between being animal brutes on one hand and civilised people on the other. He also thought that technological progress and civilisation corrupted people.

Thomas Hobbes (1588–1679) thought almost the opposite. He believed that nature was a terrible place for people to be. He said that life would be 'solitary, poor, nasty, brutish and short'. He thought that people in an uncivilised society would succumb to all of their worst instincts. In each person's drive to get whatever they wanted they would ignore the welfare of anyone else. In this society there would be no art, no culture and no industry. He felt that the only solution was for people to come out of the jungle and live in a society (or 'commonwealth') where they gave up their freedom to do whatever they wanted, but received a lot more protection in return.

More conversation

a) Where would you rather live? In a place where you could be a 'noble savage' or in our own world? Why?

b) If you could live in a place without any rules (no parents, teachers or police telling you what to do), what would happen to your own personality? What sort of person would you become? Would you fight more? Would you care for other people more? Would you want as much? Would you become a better person or worse person?

c) Do you agree with Rousseau or Hobbes? Do you think that most people would be at their best as 'noble savages' or in a society like ours?

d) What is more important in life? To be good, to be happy or to be successful?

e) If people start off 'good' what can be done in society to make sure we all stay good?

f) If people start of 'bad' (or at least flawed) what can be done in society to make sure we get better?

g) Are you an optimist or a pessimist about people? Or are you somewhere in the middle? If so where?

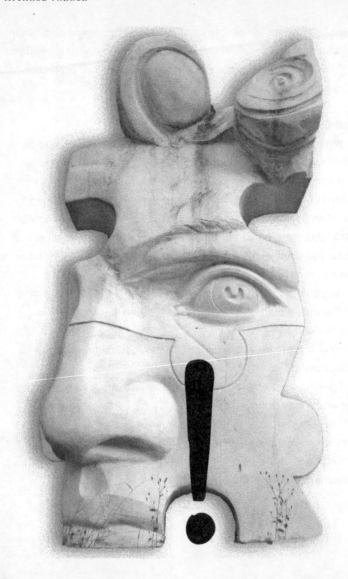

BIG IDEA 9:
When is you not you?

BACKGROUND BRIEFING

There is an ancient Greek legend about the Ship of Theseus. This fine and noble ship eventually had all of its oars replaced because they decayed. Then one by one the planks in the hull were replaced. Eventually there was no part of the ship that was made of the original material. Philosophers such as Plutarch then asked 'was it the same ship?' There are less ancient examples of this same paradox, from John Locke's sock (if he kept patching up holes with new wool until none of the old sock was left was it still the same sock?) to George Washington's axe (the head was replaced, then later the handle was replaced — so was it the same axe?)

Conversation
a) When is your old house not your house:
  a. If you get new armchairs, is it the same house?
  b. If you renovate the kitchen, is it the same house?

c. If you change all the furniture, is it the same house?

d. If you change the roof, is it the same house?

e. If you renovate the whole house, is it the same house?

f. If you replace all of the bricks, is it the same house?

g. If you do *all* of these things to your house, is it the same house?

h. If the builder who made your new house stole all of the old throwaway items and put them together in the same way on a block of land a suburb away, is *this* really your house?

i. When does something stop being the same house and start being a different house?

P.S.

Your cells change. Some of the cells in your stomach last only a few days. The surface layer of your skin lasts about two weeks before it is replaced. A red blood cell lasts about three months and cells in organs such as the liver last about a year or two. Bones are gradually replaced so that all the cells are new every ten years or so (not all at once but rather a few every day, so that very few cells are there for more than ten years) Some muscle cells around the ribs can last 15 years.

More conversation

a) Will you have the same body in ten years' time or not?

b) Is it the physical cells or the 'recipe book' (the DNA instructions) that define your body?

c) Why are you the same person that you were last year?

d) If you learn a whole lot of new maths tomorrow will you be the same person as you are today? Why?

e) If you convert to a different religion tomorrow will you be the same person in a year as you are today? Why?

f) If you lose your legs tomorrow, will you be the same person in a year as you are today? Why?

g) If you change your mind about a big issue (eg you decide to vote Liberal instead of Labor or Republican instead of Democrat) are you still the same person? Why?

h) If a rock falls on your head tomorrow and you forget everything that happened to you from the age of five to now, would you be the same person tomorrow as you are today? Why?

i) If you decide you actually dislike all of your closest friends tomorrow, and go out to make new ones, are you the same person? Why?

j) If ALL of these things happened to you at once, would you be the same person in a week's time? Why?

P.S.

A number of philosophers such as Plato and Descartes (1596–1650) held that it is the soul that keeps someone's identity together. John Locke (1632–1704) on the other hand wrote that it was someone's 'consciousness' that held them together from year to year. People's thoughts and beliefs could change, but their consciousness would remain the same.

David Hume (1711–1776) had a more radical suggestion. He thought that personal identity (or your ego) was an illusion. If he had lived in the twentieth century, he probably would have thought that your ego was like a movie. A 'movie' is just a set of separate still images on a movie reel. However, when played very fast one after the other, they create the impression that there is a single moving image — the film. Hume thought that the ego was just a set of sense impressions from the world played one after the other. Together they created a sense of personal identity, although this is in fact an illusion.

More conversation

a) Do any/all of the following things keep you as the same person:

    a. your memories?

    b. your soul?

    c. your consciousness?

    d. your attitudes?

BIG IDEA 10: What is it like to be a bat?

a) What does your pet dog or cat think about? Can it think about food or playing if it doesn't know any words? Describe what it is like inside your dog/cat's head when it is 'thinking' about food.

b) When a dog learns commands like 'sit' and 'come' is it learning to understand speech?

c) When dogs bark to each other are they 'speaking' a dog language? In what way?

d) Dogs' sense of sight is not very good, but their sense of smell is very good. Humans are the reverse. Can you describe what it is like to be a dog going for a walk in a park?

P.S.

Thomas Nagel (1937–) once asked what it was like to be a bat. He explained that bats 'see' in a completely different way to people. What they do is shriek, then detect the reflections that their soundwaves make on objects. Their brains interpret these echoes to work out distance, size, and whether something is moving. This is called 'echolocation' and it is the main way that bats work out the outside world.

Thomas Nagel pointed out that it was just about impossible to really imagine what it is like to be a bat. But his main point was that bats (and people) had to be 'conscious'. This was because the bat had to be experiencing *something* — there was something that it felt like to be a bat.

This is linked to the concept of 'qualia'. This idea is that experiences (such as the taste of a milkshake or the pain of a headache) are things that you really do have and are subjective to you.

More conversation

a) Close your eyes and make some sound. Then pretend to be a bat and try to imagine the world around you as reflected from the echoes of your voice. Can you imagine doing it?

b) Can you imagine what it is like to be a bat? Or is it impossible?

c) What is the difference between a bat using sonar to work out the layout of a cave and a computer using sonar to work out the layout of a cave? What does the bat have that the computer doesn't?

d) If you taste a fantastic milkshake, can you really explain the taste to someone else? Or is the 'qualia' (see above) of tasting a milkshake something trapped inside you? Can you be sure that your parents taste the milkshake in the same way as you? How?

e) Are you 'conscious' of being a human being? Is a bat 'conscious' of being a bat?

BIG IDEA 11:
Should we own a pet?

a) Does a dog have a good if life it is fed, loved, walked, brushed, and kept apart from other dogs for its whole life (apart from occasionally meeting other dogs in the street)? Why?

b) Does a dog have a good life if it is fed, loved, walked and kept alone for most of each day while the family is at work and school? Why?

c) Does a cat have a good life if it is kept in comfort inside a flat while its owner is at work? Why?

d) Does it matter whether dogs or cats have a great life? Is it more important that they provide enjoyment for people?

e) If people didn't own pets, then most dogs and cats wouldn't be born (because their parents get bred so that their babies can be sold). Is it better that these dogs and cats weren't born? Why?

f) Should dogs and cats be sold, or only given away? Why?

g) Should a bird be kept in a cage or a fish be kept in a tank? What is it gaining? What is it losing?

h) Is it hypocritical to worry about whether a budgie is having a nice time in a cage and then eat a chicken for dinner? Why/why not?

P.S.

Gary L Francione (1954–) states that pet ownership is not a good idea because many of us treat the animals like our property, not our friends. He states that animals are produced 'like bolts in a factory'. He says that even though some people treat their animals well, many people don't and that the law allows you to treat animals badly (eg by hitting them or underfeeding them). On the other hand the American Humane Association considers that owning pets is fine, as long as the bond between the animals and their owners is 'to the mutual benefit of both'.

Others suggest that keeping animals is a good way for children to learn about empathy and care for others. In addition some animals, particularly dogs, can teach us lessons about enthusiasm and loyalty.

More conversation

a) Do you think that pets are our 'property' like our toys? Would it be bad if pets were our property? Why?

b) Is desexing a dog or a cat against its rights? What would be the dangers if pets were *not* desexed?

c) What do you think that pets can teach people?

d) Is it fair to feed meat to pets when so many people in the world are starving?

BIG IDEA 12:
Curly paradoxes

BACKGROUND BRIEFING

Several of the paradoxes below (the tortoise, the frog and the arrow) come from the Ancient Greek philosopher Zeno of Elea.

Try to work out each of the paradoxes below. Don't worry if you can't — the fun is trying to get your head around them.

The tortoise and Achilles

This is the most famous of Zeno's paradoxes. A tortoise and Achilles decide to have a race. Achilles is Greek demigod, hero and man of war, so the tortoise feels at a disadvantage. The tortoise asks for a head start. He is allowed a minute to get himself as far ahead of Achilles as he can. He makes it five metres. However, Achilles finds he cannot win the race. He gets himself to the five-metre point, but finds that the tortoise has moved ahead of him. So he runs to that point and finds that the tortoise has got ahead of him again. So he runs to that new point and finds the tortoise still ahead of him.

Indeed, this race can go on forever with Achilles always catching up, but never able quite to get to the tortoise.

How can this be true? How can it be false?

The frog

This is another one of Zeno's paradoxes. If a frog can jump halfway across a pond onto a lilypad in the first jump, then half of that distance in the second jump, and half of that distance in the third jump, how many jumps would it take to jump across the lilypad? The answer is he would never get there. Because he would have jumped ½, then ¾, then ⅞, then ¹⁵⁄₁₆, but there would always still be *some* distance between him and the other side of the pond.

How can this be true? How can it be false?

Some curly lying statements

a) This statement is false.

b) I always lie.

c) i) The statement below is true.
   ii) The statement above is false.

BIG IDEA 13:
More curly paradoxes

The surprise test

In English on Monday, Mr Smith announces that there will be a surprise quiz on Shakespeare quotes one day this week. Immediately Julian starts packing his bags away.

'What are you doing?' says Mr Smith.

'Packing up,' replies Julian, 'because the quiz can't be any day this week.'

'Why not?' asks Mr Smith, a little irritated.

'Well the quiz can't be on Friday. Because if that was the case, by Thursday afternoon, it would no longer be a surprise — we'd know it was the next day.'

'Well the quiz could be any day between today and Thursday,' snaps Mr Smith.

'No it couldn't,' says Julian. 'The quiz can't be on Friday. Which means that on Wednesday night, the only time you can give us the quiz is on Thursday. So it wouldn't be a surprise. And if the test can't be on Thursday, it has to be

Tuesday or Wednesday... but on Tuesday night that means it has to be Wednesday. And so on. Which means that there can't be a test.'

'Fine,' says Mr Smith. He reaches into his bag and pulls out a wad of papers. 'Get out your pens. The quiz is right now.'

The class groans and mutters angrily. Julian looks suddenly worried. 'Oops,' he says. 'That was a surprise.'

Was Julian right? Could there be a surprise test? How?

The arrow

Zeno suggests that arrows can't move. This is because in any one moment of time (think of a photo taken of the one moment) the arrow is in a particular place in space. It is not moving to where it is going. It is not moving from where it has come from. It is frozen in that moment. Now think of the moment after this, and the moment after this. They are all snapshots of a still arrow.

So, if time is made up of moments, and the arrow is still in every moment, therefore there is no motion and the arrow cannot move.

Can the arrow move? How?

The lawyer

Mrs Judge trains Oscar to be a lawyer. She says that Oscar only needs to pay her when he wins a case. However, Oscar decides to go off and have a career growing daffodils instead. Mrs Judge is furious at Oscar because of all of the time she has wasted and she demands payment. Oscar replies 'You will never get money.

Because I was only going to pay you when I won a case, and I am never even going to start a case.'

Mrs Judge decides to sue Oscar for the money. She reasons that if she wins the case she will get the money. However, if she loses the case she will still get the money, because it means Oscar will have won his first case.

Is she right?

BIG IDEA 14:
Loving your nation/ country

BACKGROUND BRIEFING

People have identified with their individual tribe or ethnic group for thousands of years. However, the concept of the 'modern' nation as a focus of loyalty only emerged in the 1700s. Countries such as Britain developed markers such as a flags (the Union Jack) and songs. The French and American revolutions of the late 1700s further fixed the idea of nations and nationalism in people's minds. So... nations that we recognise are younger than most people think.

Conversation

a) What are some of the best things about your nation?

b) What are some of the worst things about your nation? Is it possible to love your country and also list bad things about it?

c) Do you love your country? Why?

d) Can you love a nation in the same way that you love your parents, your school or ice cream?

e) What is good and 'not so good' about having a country with just one ethnic or religious group? What is good and 'not so good' about having a country with a multiplicity of ethnic or religious groups?

f) What are the dangers of having just one type of group in a country?

g) Should a big nation (eg USA) be broken up into smaller nations (eg Texas, Idaho, New York) which might share more things in common?

h) Should smaller nations (eg Portugal, Greece, Denmark) be combined to form bigger nations which are more powerful (eg Europe)?

i) If you think that your nation has got it really right, should your nation attempt to export these things to other countries?

P.S.

Steven Weber states that nation states came about because people learnt to draw maps better from the fourteenth century and thus started to draw borders around areas of land. Eric Hobsbawn (1917–2012) holds that the French state with borders came about before the 'French' people. He points out that at the time of the French revolution, only half of the population of France even spoke any French (and only 12–13% spoke it well).

Ferdinand Tönnies (1855–1936) concentrated on two different types of society. One he said was a traditional village-based society. There would be many emotional attachments in this community. He called it a Gemeinschaft. The other society was a larger society where people did not know each other and many things were impersonal and cold. He called this Gesellschaft. Using Tönnies paradigm nationalism can be seen as promoting the values of the cold modern society and making us forget the values of a personal village type society.

More conversation

a) Imagine that we find a new continent, full of small tribes and large kingdoms. We map it. Then imagine that we draw, as carefully as we can, a set of borders around the continent so that there are 20 new 'nations' in it. Are these really nations? What would it take for them to become nations? Should they become nations?

b) If you could organise the world again from scratch, would you organise it so that we mainly felt loyal to our:

    a. nation?

    b. local community?

    c. tribe/race?

    d. state (eg Massachusetts, New South Wales, Manitoba)?

    e. sporting team or code?

    f. planet?

Why would you do this?

BIG IDEA 15:
Owning guns

BACKGROUND BRIEFING

In some countries such as Australia most people are not permitted to own guns. If you do, it has to be for a purpose (eg farming, belonging to a gun club), be locked in a cupboard and not be too powerful. In contrast the USA includes the right to 'bear arms' (ie own guns) in its Constitution. Many people have guns in their houses so that they can 'protect themselves' in the case of burglary etc.

Conversation

a) Why do different people want to own guns? How many of these reasons do you think are good ones? Why?

b) People in many countries have a 'right' to

speak freely, to vote etc. Should people have a 'right' to own guns? Why/why not?

c) What do you think would happen in society if:

a. everyone owned a gun?

b. no-one owned a gun?

c. only the police owned guns?

d. only criminals owned guns?

d) What sort of city/town/village would you like to live in? One with a lot of guns, only a few or none?

e) Do you think people should be able to own a gun to defend themselves against:

a. someone who breaks into their house?

b. a government who tries to 'take over' the country and stop it from being a democracy?

f) Some people use guns for the wrong reason (eg to shoot a lot of innocent people). Is this a good reason to stop a lot of people from owning guns?

g) Should people be able to carry the following weapons in the street:

a. knives?

b. bows and arrows?

c. guns?

    d. grenades?

    e. rocket powered missiles? (although these would be quite heavy)

P.S.

Many people in the USA point out that the 'Founding Fathers' (ie the people who wrote the Constitution) wanted Americans to own guns and therefore wrote it into the Constitution.

The Small Arms survey of 2007 ranked countries on the basis of how many guns were owned per hundred people. Some of the results are listed below.

1st	United States of America	94.3 guns per hundred people
2nd	Yemen	54.8 guns per hundred people
3rd	Switzerland	45.7 guns per hundred people
42nd	Australia	15 guns per hundred people
88th	England and Wales	6.2 guns per hundred people.

Statistics in this area can show different pictures. For example one study in Australia (done by Harvard University) found that killings with guns dropped by 59% in the years after the 1996 gun ban. The researchers at Harvard University also found by looking at 26 other developed countries that the more firearms there are, the more killings there are. In the USA the murder rate is about 15 times higher than other wealthy countries. However there are examples from the 1960s and 1970s (eg Hawaii and Washington DC) that show that after firearms were restricted, the murder rate actually went up.

More conversation

a) Why do you think the USA has so many more guns than other countries? Is the US safer/more free as a result?

b) Why could a crime rate go *up* after firearms are restricted?

c) If you were the government would you:

    a. make guns available to everyone?

    b. let people buy guns after they had been checked to make sure they weren't criminals?

    c. only let farmers own guns?

    d. ban guns altogether?

    e. do something else?

Self Portrait

BIG IDEA 16:
But is it art?

BACKGROUND BRIEFING

Imagine that your family have been made the next curators of the National Gallery. You will be given several hundred million dollars to buy new and wonderful art. However, people start to approach you with all sorts of unusual artistic offers. You also have to have a family conference to work out what art even *is*.

Conversation

a) Bob comes to you with an authentic piece of crumpled paper. On it is a twenty-second scribble that Leonardo Da Vinci did to plan the Mona Lisa. He then threw it in the bin where a cleaner picked it up, and handed it down through his family for generations. Is this art?

b) Sally brings you a printout of the Mona Lisa. Is this art?

c) You tell Sally that printing out the Mona Lisa is not art. She takes out a pen and draws a moustache on the printout. Is it now art?

d) Jackson comes to you with a painting that he has done in which he has dripped and poured paint on a canvas on the floor. This is all he has done. Is this art?

e) Mark brings you several canvases which depict stripes. One in particular has three yellow and rose stripes. Are they art?

f) Robert brings you several works that are white on white. Is this art?

g) Selma comes to you with a whole train carriage (which took a lot of getting into the lobby). She broke into a railway yard and spray-painted it with a thousand tags. Is this art?

h) Ferdinand, the architect of the National Art Gallery, says that the building you are already in is a piece of art. Then he asks you to give him more money for it. Is the building art?

i) Jean Claude comes to you and offers to wrap the entire National Gallery in plastic. Is this art?

j) Your grandmother brings you a very nice desk lamp she has used for 50 years. Is it art?

k) Marcel comes into your office carrying a urinal from a toilet down the street. He puts it against the wall and says it is now art. Is it art?

l) Arisa, from Thailand, comes to you with some abstract canvases. She says that they come from her elephant farm in Thailand where the elephants all paint. Are they art?

P.S.

Fine art can be anything that is designed to produce an aesthetic response. Art can be defined as human-made things that are designed to be appreciated for their own sake.

A wider definition is that art is anything that is made in humans, even though this could include cars or rubbish dumps.

a) Which do you think is a better definition of art? Why?

BIG IDEA 17: Human invention

a) Imagine that you could go back in time and stop things from being invented. Pick out five human inventions and imagine, one by one, that you stop them ever coming into existence. (Perhaps choose them by looking around the house or looking outside.) What does your life look like? What does the world look like?

b) Go back in time and stop the following things from being invented/discovered:

    a. the wheel

    b. fire

    c. the number system (ie 0, 1, 2, 3, 4 etc)

    d. spoken language

    e. the printing press

    f. the microchip

    g. the clock

    h. money

What does the world look like without each of *these* inventions/ discoveries? Can the world progress without any one of them?

Would we be happier if any one of these things had not been invented/discovered?

c) What do you think the biggest, most important single invention is? Why?

d) What is good (or bad) about each of the following inventions? Rank them in order of importance. See what the other members of your family think.

a. guns

b. telephones

c. computers

d. the compass

e. television

f. antibiotics

g. anaesthetic

h. nuclear bombs

BIG IDEA 18:
Our history

a) Draw a 'timeline' with your own life on it. Put the year you were born on one end and this year at the other end. Now draw on the timeline the biggest events in your life. Talk with your parents/children about what the biggest events were and why they were the biggest events.

b) Draw a timeline with the year 1700 at one end and this year at the other end. What big events can you put on the timeline (don't worry if you don't know the years, just put them wherever you think they might go)?

c) Draw a timeline from the Big Bang start of the universe to now. This line should go from 14 billion BC to now. What events do you think should go on this timeline, and where should they go? Don't worry if you don't know exactly where they go — just put them where you think they might go. What events would you like to find some more about?

P.S.

The following websites may help if you are interested in fleshing your timetables out. There is a lot of detail in some of them.

www.datesandevents.org/events-timelines/14-american-history-timeline.htm

www.bbc.co.uk/history/interactive/timelines/

www.aushistorytimeline.com

http://resources.schoolscience.co.uk/STFC/bang/bang.htm

www.timemaps.com/history

www.dummies.com/how-to/content/a-timeline-of-world-history.html

BIG IDEA 19:
Our human future

a) Imagine the future. What might it be like in:

a. fifty years?
b. a thousand years?
c. a million years?

b) What are the best and most exciting futures? What are the worst and most scary futures?

c) What would we have to do *now* to increase the chance that the exciting futures happen, and not the scary ones?

P.S.

Carl Sagan the astronomer wrote about the future of humanity:

> *'The civilization now in jeopardy is all humanity. In our tenure of this planet we've accumulated dangerous evolutionary baggage — propensities for aggression and ritual, submission to leaders, hostility to outsiders — all of which puts our survival in some doubt.*
>
> *But we've also acquired compassion for others, love for our children and desire to learn from history and experience, and a great soaring passionate intelligence — the clear tools for our continued survival and prosperity. Which aspects of our nature will prevail is uncertain, particularly when our visions and prospects are bound to one small part of the small planet Earth.*
>
> *But up there in the immensity of the Cosmos, an inescapable perspective awaits us... National boundaries are not evident when we view the Earth from space. Fanatical ethnic or religious or national chauvinisms are a little difficult to maintain when we see our planet as a fragile blue crescent fading to become an inconspicuous point of light against the bastion and citadel of the stars. Travel is broadening.*
> (*'Cosmos'* Random House 1980 p 318)

More conversation

a) How does your vision of the future compare to Carl Sagan's? Are you more optimistic or pessimistic than him?

b) What is Carl Sagan's big idea? What do you think about Carl Sagan's big idea?

c) What happens when you look at a picture of the Earth from space? Do 'national chauvinisms' fade for you? Or does something else happen for you?

d) Look up the following photograph: http://en.wikipedia.org/wiki/File:Pale_Blue_Dot.png

It is a photograph taken of Earth from the Voyager spacecraft in 1990 at a distance of six billion miles from Earth. Earth is the blue dot halfway down the brown line on the right hand side of the photo. It takes up one pixel. Does it make the Earth feel more precious? Does it make the Earth feel small? Or something else?

BIG IDEA 20:
Love

a) How is love for your favourite TV programme different to love for your family?

b) Can you 'love' your friends? How is this different to love for your parents?

c) Can you love people you don't know, such as an actor or a pop star?

d) Can you love animals (eg your pet dog) as much as people? Can you love them *more*? Can your pet love you back?

e) How is a love of God different to a love of people? How is it the same?

f) Can people have a maximum amount of love? If your parents had another child, would they have to divide up their love so that they loved you a little less, or would they find more love? Explain.

g) Couples often 'fall in love' when they are young, and then stay together for 50 years. Is their love the same at the end of this time as it was at the beginning? If your grandparents are still together, how do they love each other?

h) Imagine a society where instead of people marrying one person, groups of eight people got together and 'married' as a unit. How would their love be similar and different to love of one other person? Is this a better way to marry?

i) People who join the army and face death with their platoon talk about loving their army mates as much as their family. Is this the same type of love, or different?

j) How is 'love for life' different to 'love for people'?

k) Is it possible to 'love' your country or the whole human race?

l) Americans are often described as 'freedom loving'. What sort of love is this? Is this stronger than love for friends or family?

m) Is love just a series of chemical and physical reactions (heart beating faster, flushing of face, release of the chemical dopamine? Or is it something more?

n) People talk about the love of thinking.

o) What would the world look like without any love at all in it? Would it work? Would it work *better* than our world?

p) Can animals love each other?

q) If a computer 'learned' how to think, could it 'learn' how to love?

P.S.

The English language has one word 'love' that covers a lot of connected, but different emotions. The Ancient Greeks (and Romans) had different words for the different emotions, which allowed them to think about them separately much more easily. They included:

Agape: This means a general, spiritual love for your fellow human beings, or for life or your God. We also see this type of love in the Bible; (eg Matthew 22.37 reported Christ as saying 'Love your neighbour as you love yourself.')

Storge: This is a brotherly/sisterly love felt by people who have a strong common connection. This could include being in the same army platoon, or school year group, or by people who share a strong common experience.

Philia: This is the deep bond of love for members of your family or your closest friends. (Sometimes *storge* and *philia* are used together).

Eros: This is passionate love — the romantic, all eclipsing love of meeting someone that you fall 'head over heels' in love with. It is the type of love where your day is spent waiting for a text or a Facebook message from someone. This is the type of love that most songs and films are about. Many Greeks actually saw an extreme form of this love (Mania) as an affliction or a punishment.

Neuroscientists have been able to identify what chemicals in the brain are involved when people experience love. *Dopamine*, *testosterone*, *serotonin* and *adrenalin* are all connected with passionate, romantic love (the hot flushes, racing heart etc). *Oxytocin* and *vasopressin* are connected to the 'attachment' version of love where there is long-term bonding.

More conversation

a) If you could only have two of the Ancient Greek types of love, which two would you have?

b) How does having the different Greek words for 'love' help you think about love at all? Does it change any of the conversations you had about the questions above?

c) If you injected a lot of dopamine and serotonin into someone on a subway, and they immediately fell in love with the person sitting opposite them, would this be real love? Why?

d) If you injected dopamine and serotonin into a couple who were about to get divorced and they fell back in love with one another, would you have you done a good thing?

e) Do chemicals produce love? Or does love produce chemicals?

BIG IDEA 21: Freedom of speech

BACKGROUND BRIEFING

Freedom of speech is one of the most important rights in any free society, particularly a democratic society. Without it a society would probably turn quickly into a police state where individual people had few rights at all. It is so important that it is a key part of the First Amendment to the United States Constitution: *Congress shall make no law...* abridging the freedom of speech. It is also part of the United Nations Declaration of Human Rights (Article 19) '*Everyone has the right to freedom of opinion and expression; this right includes freedom to hold opinions without interference.*'

Conversation

a) Imagine that a new President/Prime Minister came to power and banned freedom of speech. People could be jailed for saying anything bad about him or his government. What would happen next, and next and next? What would the country look like in five years?

b) In our society, are people allowed to say whatever they like? Do we have freedom of speech?

c) Imagine that one person owned most of the newspapers and television stations. Imagine too that there was a presidential election with two candidates. The owner decided to write only good things about one candidate and only bad things about the other candidate. Would this country have freedom of speech?

d) Imagine that the owner of the television stations and newspapers decided to RUN for President/Prime Minister and the papers/stations ran only positive stories about him. Would this country have freedom of speech?

e) Imagine that a man named Julian set up a website that allowed people to upload secret documents from the military, spy agencies, governments etc. He says that this is okay because of freedom of speech. Do you agree with him? Or are there some documents that should stay secret?

f) How easy would it be to destroy freedom of speech in your country?

g) Is there more freedom of speech on the internet? Should there be?

h) Is there freedom of speech in your house? Should there be?

i) Is there freedom of speech in your school? Should there be?

P.S.

There have been quite a few restrictions to freedom of speech rights. 'Defamation' laws forbid false statements that injure people or businesses. Laws of business forbid statements that are designed to mislead or be fraudulent. Many countries have made it illegal to talk about committing a crime (eg assassinating the President/Prime Minister) even if you don't do anything about it.

a) Should you be able to say or write anything you like using freedom of speech as your defence? For example should you be able to:

    a. post terrible lies about what your enemy got up to at a party on Saturday night?

    b. post the terrible truth about what your enemy got up to at a party on Saturday night?

    c. say that the President/Prime Minister had an affair or was on drugs, when you have no evidence for it at all.

    d. threaten violence against the President/Prime Minister?

    e. write that a particular race (eg white people, black people, green people) are terrible vermin who are stupid and should be stamped out?

    f. tell shareholders in your company that it is making a profit when in fact your company is going broke.

    g. tell the public that the bottled water your company makes is from a 'pure spring from the South of France' when in fact it comes from the tap.

What should the limits of freedom of speech be? How do you make limits on it without threatening freedom of speech itself?

BIG IDEA 22:
Cloning

BACKGROUND BRIEFING

Our genes are the recipe books inside our cells that make up what we are like. All living things have them. Cloning is what happens when those genes are copied exactly to make a 'new' life form with exactly the same recipe book. Some creatures have done it in nature for millions of years — like bacteria, insects or plants.

Humans have learnt how to clone plants and some animals, so that the 'offspring' has exactly the same genes as the parents. 'Dolly' was the first sheep cloned in this way in 1996. Since then many animals such as horses, dogs and camels have been cloned.

Conversation

a) If it turns out one type of wheat is the best and tastiest to eat, should we clone it and have whole fields of it?

b) If it turns out that one cow is the best and tastiest to eat, should it be cloned many times so that whole herd is made up of copies of this one cow?

c) The mammoth is extinct, but we have its genetic code. Should we clone it and bring it back to life? Why/why not?

d) Should we use cloning to bring back to life other species that have become extinct, or are endangered?

e) If we could get the DNA of dinosaurs, should we clone them? What would be exciting about this? What would be the dangers?

f) If our heart was failing and we could make a copy of it in the lab with a 3D printer, should we?

P.S.

Scientists in Maastrict have created a burger in the lab using cow stem cells (it cost $325 000!) If this could be commercially reproduced, it would mean that meat could be 'grown' for consumption, instead of having to breed animals.

a) Is this a good way to make meat in the future, once it gets a lot cheaper?

b) Is it kinder to grow meat this way instead of breeding animals?

c) What might be the dangers of growing meat this way?

d) Would you be happy to eat meat that was grown as meat?

P.P.S.

'Therapeutic human cloning' involves taking a cell from anywhere in the body (eg the skin) taking out the genes and putting them into a human egg. (The egg would already have had its own genes removed). This egg could then grow into an embryo. Eventually, if you let it, it could grow into a human, although this has not been tested.

a) Would it be okay to use this embryo to help cure diseases? Why/why not?

b) Would it be okay to use this embryo to create a new baby who had exactly the same genes as its mother?

BIG IDEA 23: Marxism

BACKGROUND BRIEFING

Karl Marx was a German philosopher who wrote in the mid-nineteenth century. He wrote a theory about how society worked and in particular how he thought capitalism worked. This analysis is still found to be useful by many people. He also thought that capitalism was a very poor system which he thought should be overthrown. He believed it should be replaced with a communist society. This second set of ideas is not accepted by many people in the Western world today.

Conversation

a) Imagine that you work in a factory that makes boxes. If you made 50 boxes a day, you could sell them yourself and make $50, which would be enough to live on happily. Instead you make a 60 boxes a day, which can be sold for $60. The owner of the factory gives you $50 a day and keeps the remaining $10 for himself. Do you think this is a good idea?

b) Imagine that you own a factory. You have put the money in to make the factory work. You risk losing this money if the factory fails. In this factory are 100 workers each making 60 boxes per day. Is it okay to pay them each $50 per day and keep the rest of the money ($1000 per day) yourself?

c) What is more important in keeping a factory going, the money to start it up (capital) or the work to keep it going (labour)?

P.S.

Marx called the gap between how hard a workers needs to work to live and how hard s/he actually works 'surplus value'. He believed that the factory owner or 'capitalist' steals this surplus value for himself. The way Marx phrased it is that the capitalist has 'appropriated the means of production'. He wrote in the Communist Manifesto 'Man is born free but everywhere he is in chains'. Marx also calls the factory owners/middle class 'the bourgeoisie' and the workers the 'proletariat'.

Conversation

a) Who should own the box factory?

    a. the woman who invented the idea of the box

    b. the man who owned the land and built the factory

    c. other people who offered to pay some money to buy part of the factory (shareholders)

    d. the workers who make each box

    e. a combination of the above

b) Marx felt that workers should own 'the means of production' (eg the box factory). What do you think of his view?

c) Marx thought that in practice many people only did the same repetitive boring task again and again (eg make boxes all day). He called this 'alienated labour' and thought it was a bad thing. Do you think it is a bad thing? Do you think that things could change to avoid it?

d) Which class would you rather belong to — the 'middle class' or the 'working class'? Why?

e) Do you think you can move from one class to another very easily? Why or why not?

f) Marx believed that after parents died they should not be allowed to leave their property and money to their children. Why do you think he believed this? What do you think?

g) What would happen if the government owned the box factory and paid people $50 per day to make boxes. How many boxes do you think each person would make? The same, more or less?

h) A version of Marxism was tried in a number of countries in the twentieth century. It didn't work as well as Marx hoped. Why do you think it might not have worked?

BIG IDEA 24:
Free will

BACKGROUND BRIEFING

We all think that we have free will. When we make choices we feel that we freely make them. However, many people believe that this free will is just an *illusion*, that everything has already been set in place and we are just puppets acting out a show. (There is a little more about the philosophy behind this in 'P.S.' below).

Conversation

a) Imagine that free will is an illusion. Imagine that you are just a puppet being controlled by the great Thunder God Thor and are acting out a script that was written in Thunder Heaven. Could this be true? How would it make you feel? Would you stop trying to do anything if you found out it was true?

b) It may be that in your future you become famous, rich and successful. You may make the Australian Cricket team or you may become a Hollywood star, or you may not. Do you think that

this is already set, or will it change depending on what choices you make?
If you are going to fall down and break your ankle this afternoon, is this already set? Or not?

c) If you are going to have an argument with your best friend this afternoon, is this already set?

d) Should you work to try to make a difference in your life, or is it all just determined?

e) One day (presumably in many, many years' time) you will die, as all people do. Do you think that this date is already set?

f) Imagine you could work out where every atom in the world is and where it is going to go next. We are made of atoms. If we could work this out, would we have any free will, or is it all just determined? Why do you say this?

P.S.

Determinists are those who do not believe in free will. Causal Determinists such as Benedictus De Spinoza say that in the physical world everything that happens is caused by something before it, which in turn is caused by something before it. If you could take a complete enough picture of what it was like at a past time, you could therefore work out exactly what things will be like at a future time. This leaves very little space for free will. Theological Determinists believe that a god has already determined everything that has happened and we cannot change it. Many scientists also hold that the nature of time is that the future is already there. If our future is 'already there', then we do not have the free will to change it.

Libertarians on the other hand believe that there is free will. Some do this by saying that decisions are taken by a 'soul' in the brain. They say that this 'overrides' physical acts that may be predicted. Philosophers such as Robert Kane speak of people having 'ultimate responsibility'. Others (such as Walter Heisenberg) believe that right down at a very small level (atomic and quantum) you cannot predict physical acts anyway.

More conversation

a) If people do not have free will can we morally blame them for being unethical?

b) If people do not have free will can we punish them for committing terrible crimes?

c) On a 'softer' level, people's careers and lives may be determined by their parents, their social position and their intelligence. Does this mean that someone is 'determined' to succeed or fail?

d) What chance does an impoverished beggar in an Indian slum have of becoming a computer genius, the owner of a company or a University Professor? Does this mean that the beggar is destined to have a bad life?

BIG IDEA 25:
Political parties

a) Many parents support one political party. Find out if your parents support one party [Labor/Liberal or Republican/Democrat]. Why do they support this party? Have they always supported this party?

b) Do your parents support the party no matter who the leader is, or do they make their judgement on the basis of the leader? Why?

c) Imagine that the leader of the party your parents do not support turned up in your living room and asked for your vote. Get your parents to explain what they would say and why. Why do your parents not support him/her?

d) Should children have the same political beliefs as their parents? Why? Do children often end up having the same beliefs as their parents? Why?

e) If children had very different political beliefs than their parents, should their parents be disappointed in them? Why/why not?

f) Many parents decide who to vote for at each election. They are called 'swinging voters'. Find out if your parents are swinging voters. If they are, how do they choose how to vote at each election? Is it a good thing to be a swinging voter? Should everyone be a swinging voter? Or no-one? Why/why not?

P.S.: LEFT WING/RIGHT WING

Most political parties see themselves as left wing or right wing. The left wing believes that a government should get involved in many areas (environment, work laws etc) in order to try to achieve greater fairness and social justice. They oppose social disadvantage.

The right wing believes that individual people should be free to run their lives and their businesses in ways that they choose (within reason). They believe that freedom to act makes people more motivated, which allows more to get done.

These are gross simplifications. Most parties take some elements from both the left wing and the right wing. The terms 'left wing' and 'right wing' came from what side of the room people sat during the first French Parliament from 1789–1799.

Conversation

a) Would you describe yourself as more left wing or more right wing? Why?

b) Would you describe your parents as more left wing or more right wing? Why?

BIG IDEA 26: Democracy

BACKGROUND BRIEFING

Representative democracy is a system where all of the individuals in a country get to choose the government. The people do this by *voting* between competing political parties who say they can run the country the best. This voting occurs every few years at elections.

Conversation

a) Imagine that your school had a Principal and an 'Opposition Principal' who criticises everything the Principal says. Every four years the school gets to choose which Principal they will have for the next four years. Would this system be more democratic? Would this system work? Why/why not?

b) Do you think we should live in a monarchy, where just the King or Queen rule and they hand power on to their children? Why/Why not? Can you think of any advantages of this system?

c) Do you think we should live in a society where the army rules and makes sure that no-one opposes them by shooting dissenters? Why/why not?

d) Do you think we should live in a society where one man/woman takes over the government and rules for the rest of his/her life without elections? Why/why not?

e) Imagine someone who had ruled a country for 30 years without anyone opposing him/her.

   a. Do you think s/he would be a good person?
   b. Do you think s/he could make good decisions?
   c. Do you think people would be able to tell him/her they were wrong about something?

f) Imagine you became the leader of a country and you decided that you wanted to destroy democracy so that your family could have power for a century. Plan what to do. What would you do to:

   a. the newspapers?
   b. the army?
   c. the people who disagreed with you?
   d. telephones and social media?
   e. the courts?
   f. the powerful people who ran businesses and were rich?

P.S.

Ancient Athens (where democracy originated) had a more direct form of democracy. Citizens were directly involved in making laws (by turning up to meeting places) instead of voting for other people to make them. People were also chosen randomly to fill important government jobs. Ancient Sparta had a form of voting in which elections were held by shouting. The candidate who got the loudest shout from the crowd after his name was called was elected.

a) What do you think our society would be like if we could vote on every law as it came up, not just for the government once every few years? Would you participate? Why?

b) What do you think our society would be like if we picked people randomly to fill government positions every few years. Would your parents be very good at it? Would this be better than our system or worse? Why?

c) Can you see anything good about shouting for a candidate?

d) In Athens you had to be a 'citizen' in order to vote. To be a citizen you had to own property (and be a man, over 20 years old and not a slave). Is it a good idea to only let property owners vote? Why/why not? Why do you think that they did it?

e) Imagine a country where there were elections every few years. However, there were no newspapers and people could be thrown in gaol for speaking against the government. Is this still a democracy, or not?

f) At the moment the voting age is 18 years. Should younger people who want to vote be able to?

BIG IDEA 27:
Immortality (on Earth)

a) Would you like to live forever? Why or why not? What would you do if you were immortal?

b) What would happen to you if you lived forever?

    a. Would you get bored?

    b. Would you miss people?

    c. Would your personality change?

    d. Would your relationships with other people change?

    e. Would you become extremely successful?

    f. Would you become very smart or wise?

c) Would you want to live forever if all of your family and friends could live forever with you?

d) What would happen to human society if people lived forever, or at least for a very long time (for example a hundred thousand years)?

e) Would you like to have the ability to live forever, if at any time you could press a button that allowed you to die?

f) What do you think would be the ideal lifespan?

P.S.

Research into living forever (or at least for much longer than currently possible) breaks into several strands. There is the fighting of biological aging at the cellular level. There is studying the unusual lifecycles of animals such as jellyfish, which appear to change from one form to another, and so are, in effect, immortal. Others study cryonics, which is the freezing of people who die now in the hope that they can be revived in the future when the technology is more available. Other possibilities focus on mind transference, from your brain to some other medium (often a digital environment such as a virtual reality zone).

More conversation

a) If scientists could replace your organs one by one, replace all of your aging muscles, and stop your brain from decaying, you could live for thousands of years. Would you take this option?

b) Scientists in the future might be able to record everything about you and download it into a virtual reality programme. This collection of data would think it was you and would live in an environment that felt totally real. This programme could go on forever with 'you' in it. (The programme could also work so that a day felt like a year to the people inside it). Would you do this? Would this be getting a form of immortality?

c) Some people have already been frozen 'cryogenically' after they died so that they can be 'woken up' in the future when technology may allow them to keep living. This is a controversial technology. Would you consider using it?

BIG IDEA 28:
How smart can kids be?

a) Can kids be smarter than their parents?

b) What would make parents smarter than their kids?

c) What do kids know more about than their parents? What do parents know more about than their kids?

d) What is 'being smart' or 'being intelligent?' What does it actually *mean*?

e) How can you tell if someone is currently smart or intelligent? Could there be people in your class who are really smart without you knowing?

f) Can you get smarter? *How* would you try to get smarter?

g) Is everyone smart in some way? How?

P.S.

Jean Piaget (1896–1980) wrote about humans moving from 'concrete' thinking as children to more 'abstract' thinking as they became older.

Howard Gardner (1943–) claimed in 1983 that there was not just one phenomenon called 'intelligence' but instead there were 'multiple intelligences'. They included:

- verbal linguistic — ability with words and language
- logic mathematical — reasoning, critical thinking, mathematics
- musical — sensitivity to sound, tones and music
- spatial — the ability to judge elements of space with the mind's eye — visualising
- bodily/kinaesthetic — moving, handling your body, using tools
- interpersonal — the ability to co-operate by being sensitive to other people; their moods, temperament etc
- intrapersonal — how well you can think about yourself and know yourself?
- naturalistic — how well you can relate information linked to your surroundings?

Carol Dweck (1946–) writes about people having 'fixed mindsets' or 'growth mindsets' about their abilities. People with fixed mindsets have a static sense of their own intelligence and are concerned with how smart they look. People with 'growth mindsets' seek to improve and learn from setbacks. They have a fluid sense of their own intelligence/brain as a 'muscle' that can be strengthened.

More conversation

a) Which of Gardner's multiple Intelligences are you best at right now? Which ones could you get better at? What about the other members of your family?

b) What do you think about the idea of '*multiple* intelligences' instead of just one?

c) Some researchers have suggested there should be a new type of multiple intelligence called 'existential intelligence' which is the willingness to think about big questions. Do you agree with this? Why?

d) Do you think that children can think 'abstractly'? What age do you think you started to do it? How could you make people do it when they are younger?

e) Do you think you have a 'fixed mindset' according to 'Carol Dweck' or a 'growth mindset'? Which one would you rather have? What would you have to do to yourself to get a stronger 'growth mindset'?

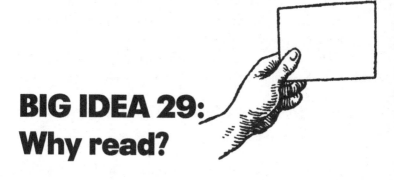

BIG IDEA 29:
Why read?

a) What would the world look like if no-one could read? What would schools, businesses and governments look like?

b) What if your school taught using only videos and YouTube? Would this be better or worse? Why?

c) A thousand years ago, almost nobody could read. What do you think that life was like for those people?

d) Do you like to read? Why or why not? Do your parents like to read? Why or why not?

e) What are your favourite books? What are your parents' favourite books?

f) What does reading a book give you that watching a movie doesn't? What does watching a movie give you that reading doesn't?

P.S.

Some of the reasons suggested for reading over the years include:

- It's fun and entertaining.
- It's like a form of virtual reality — when you get into reading, you stop seeing word after word, but instead get sucked into the story and really feel like you are there.
- It helps you understand other people — by getting into the minds of other characters, you can sympathise with real people.
- It helps you learn about our world (and beyond) — places, situations, ideas etc.
- It improves your verbal ability, your word power, your imagination, your brain, your memory and your power in society.
- It teaches you some of the greatest, most interesting and most important things that people have learned over the past few thousand years. It is the knowledge of ages handed down to you.
- In good books the way that the words are put together is beautiful or really interesting — like a piece of art or music.

Harold Bloom in 'How to Read and Why' says that we should read to help construct, create and make ourselves. He says we read to increase our wit, our imagination and our sense of intimacy. He also says that we read to 'search for a difficult pleasure'.

More conversation

a) Which of the reasons above do you agree with? Are there any you don't agree with?

b) Could reading really help 'create' ourselves, as Harold Bloom suggests? And what is good about a 'difficult pleasure?' (see also Big Idea 28: How smart can kids be?)

c)   What do you think might be the most important book ever written? Why? (You may need to go onto the internet to find that out, or read a book.)

d)   Can some books be better than others, or is it all up to each reader's opinion?

BIG IDEA 30:
What is life?

a) Imagine that an alien has come down to earth and said that it doesn't know what 'life' is. It points to a rock and asks whether it is alive. You say 'no'. It then points to a tree and asks if it is alive. You say 'yes'. It asks what the difference is. What do you tell it?

b) The alien points to your friend and asks if it is alive. You say 'yes'. It then points to a character in a film you are watching and asks if it is alive. You say 'no'. It asks what the difference is. What do you tell it?

c) The alien points to your pet dog and asks if it is alive. You say 'yes'. It then points to a wind-up mechanical mouse you have and asks if it is alive. You say 'no'. It asks what the difference is. What do you tell it?

d) The alien then opens up his chest and shows that it is mechanical — like an extremely advanced robot. It asks if *it* is alive. What do you tell it?

e) Are *you* alive? Why? How do you know?

f) How would you work out if something on Earth is alive or not?

    a. an animal

    b. a tree

    c. a wooden table

    d. bacteria

    e. a virus

    f. a computer virus

    g. a seed

    h. an egg

    i. a cup

    j. coral

    k. fire

    l. a person's memory

    m. the ideas in a book

g) Is the Earth alive? Is the universe alive?

h) Do you think animals or plants are more alive? Why/why not?

i) Is a person more alive than bacteria or a piece of pond slime?

j) Is a very healthy athlete who just won the 100 metres sprint at the Olympics more alive that a 90-year old person who is just about to draw his last breath? Or are they just as alive as each other at that moment?

k) Is there any such thing as 'more' alive? Or is it just 'alive' and 'not alive'.

l) Could a very powerful computer ever become alive? Why/why not?

m) Could the characters inside a very powerful computer game ever become alive? What if the characters inside the game were programmed to 'think'?

BIG IDEA 31:
Friendship

a) Who are your best friends?

b) What do you like about your best friends?

c) *Why* are they your best friends?

d) How many best friends can you have? Why do you say this?

e) Are there things that your friends can give you that your family cannot? What are they?

f) Are you a *good* friend to your friends? What does it take to be a good friend?

g) Should you hang around with friends who are always getting into trouble? Why/why not?

h) Do your friends help shape you into the person you are? If so, how? Does this mean that if you have a friend in trouble you should stop being with them because they will affect you for the worse?

i) If a good friend of yours was doing something dangerous (eg catching onto the back of a bus with their skateboard and being taken along for a ride) would you tell their parents? Would you try to get them to stop in some other way? What if you failed?

j) Are you responsible for your friends?

k) Is it okay to 'trade up' your best friend if you are a little bored with them and someone new who you really like comes along?

l) Can you love your friend? How is it different and similar to love of your parents or a boyfriend/girlfriend? (see also Big Idea 20: Love)

m) Can you be good friends with someone using just social media? Why/why not?

P.S.

Aristotle (in the *Nicomachean Ethics* Book VIII) states that there are three types of friendship — although you can be friends with one person for several of these reasons.

a) friendships of pleasure, where you get enjoyment yourself out of being the friend

b) friendships of utility, where the friendship is useful to you

c) friendships of virtue, where you are friends because of the person's good character

Aristotle states that most people prefer being loved to loving other people. However, a real friendship endures when the friends love each other more than they like being loved, and when they love the friend according to the friend's merit.

He also states that you can only be real friends with a small number of people, and that there are some people you can't be friends with because the power relationship is too unequal; for example parents/children, ruler/subject.

More conversation

a) Think about your own best friends. Link them to Aristotle's three types of friendship. Are they mainly friendships of pleasure, utility or virtue?

b) Do you love your friends for what they give you? Or for their own merit?

c) If your friend loves basketball and you love cricket, should you become interested in basketball just to share the interest with your friend? Should you go in search of someone who likes cricket as a friend instead?

d) Can parents and their children be friends? Why/why not?

e) Can you be best friends with your dog or your cat? Why/why not?

f) Do we need friends? Can people get on fine without them?

BIG IDEA 32:
Time paradoxes

BACKGROUND BRIEFING

A number of physicists, such as Kip Thorne, have suggested that time travel could be physically possible. It may be achieved through a combination of wormholes and understanding the concept that time slows down when you move. However, we do not have anything approaching the technology at the moment to travel in time. If we did, all sorts of bizarre things may start to happen.

Conversation

a) Imagine that you travel back in time to watch your grandparents first meet each other. Apparently, let's say, they met on a bridge over a stream. But when you get there, you are struck with how beautiful your grandmother is. You start talking to her about her job, her family etc. By the time you stop talking to her, you realise you have made her late so that she does not cross the bridge at the same time as your grandfather. They

don't meet!
   a. What happens to you now?
   b. Are you ever born?
   c. Could your grandparents meet in some other way?

b) What if instead of talking to your grandmother, you run across a road near the bridge and cause a car accident. The person in the car is killed. In shock, you look into the car and realise that it is your grandfather. He will never ever be able to meet your grandmother now.
   a. Are you ever born?
   b. If you are never born, what you are doing there?
   c. If you are never born, how can you cause the car accident that stops your grandparents from meeting?
   d. If you can't cause the accident that stops your grandparents from meeting, do they meet now? Are you born now?

c) What if you went back in time and killed Adolf Hitler as a child (or kidnapped him and took him somewhere remote)?
   a. Would Word War Two still start?
   b. What would happen to all of the people who only met because of the upheavals in Europe and the world during the 1940s?
   c. Could history be worse if Hitler had not existed?
   d. Would you take the risk of killing Hitler? Or would you leave him alone?
   e. If you left Hitler alone, would you be responsible in some way for all of the people he was responsible for killing?

d) Choose another big event (Assassination of JFK, Great Fire of London) that you might be able to change. What would be the

effect of changing it? Would you do it?

P.S.

The consequences of changing the past are so thorny that several theories have been thought up to counter the idea.

The first is the 'Novikov Self Consistency Principle' which states that anything you did in the past would become a part of history. So anything you did to try to change would be destined to failure. In the example of killing Hitler, maybe your gun would jam, or you would get held up in traffic on the way to kidnapping him.

The second is the 'multiple universes theory' (from the physicist Hugh Everett), which says that new, parallel universes are branching off all the time anyway with every decision we make. So if you stop your grandparents from meeting, a new universe opens up in which your grandparents didn't meet. You never exist in THAT universe, but you do exist in yours.

More conversation

a) Both of these theories seem unlikely, but so do the 'time travel paradoxes' from the previous conversation. Which of the two theories do you prefer? Do you have another explanation?
b) Could the paradoxes mean that time travel isn't possible?

BIG IDEA 33:
Do aliens exist?

BACKGROUND BRIEFING

There are several hundred billion stars in our galaxy and a hundred billion galaxies in our universe. It appears that many, if not most of these stars have planets around them. This is a lot of opportunity for life to arise somewhere else in the universe.

Conversation

a) Do you think that aliens exist? Why?

b) Do you want aliens to exist? Why?

c) If there were aliens how do you think that they would be similar to us? How would they be different to us?

d) Do you think that they would be more likely to be friendly or unfriendly?

e) What are some of the best films you have seen about aliens? How realistic are they and why?

f) If very simple life first evolved on Mars, and then some of it caught a ride on a comet to Earth, would that make us aliens?

P.S.

The scientist Frank Drake made up a calculation that estimated the chance of aliens existing and called it 'The Drake Equation'. It estimated the chance of various occurrences happening around the universe, such as stars having planets, planets having conditions suitable for life, life actually arising, simple life evolving into complex life, and complex life not blowing itself up. He, and other scientists such as Carl Sagan, came to the conclusion from this that there were thousands of civilisations in our galaxy alone.

SETI (the search for extra-terrestrial intelligence) has been using radio telescopes to look for messages from extra-terrestrial civilisations for four decades. (Indeed, you can use your own home computer to help them process telescope data: http://setiathome. berkeley.edu/.) So far they have found nothing but silence. Yet SETI have only analysed a fragment of the sky and the signals available, and aliens may be choosing not to emit radio signals anyway.

However, some people believe that if the universe was teeming with life we should have discovered something by now.

The Fermi Paradox was named after Enrico Fermi, and states that if aliens did exist, we should already have seen them. It backs this up by saying that the sun is quite a young star — many stars are billions of years older. This means that life evolving on many of the planets around these stars have billions of years of head start on us. They would have developed inter-stellar travel many millions or billions of years ago. Therefore, even if it takes tens of millions of years to get across the galaxy, they should have colonised, or at least visited, Earth a long time ago.

More conversation

a) Do you think that there are many extra-terrestrial civilisations, very few or none? Are you more convinced by the Drake equation or the Fermi Paradox?

b) What would it be like to be colonised by technologically superior aliens? Is it more likely to be a dream or a nightmare?

c) What do you think aliens would think about us? Would they be impressed? If you had to prove to aliens that we were worth saving, what would you show them? What would you try to hide?

d) If there are no aliens, and Earth has the only life in the universe, how does this make you feel? Does it make you feel big or small? What does it say about how we should look after the Earth?

BIG IDEA 34:
Imagine a world
where... .

a) Imagine a world where everyone could read each other's minds. What would it be like? How would it be different to ours? Would you prefer to live there or here?

b) Imagine a world where everyone could zap from one place to another in the world instantly. How would it be different to ours? Would you prefer to live there or here?

c) Imagine a world where everyone could take a pill to be happy all of the time. What would it be like? How would it be different to our world? Would you rather live there or here?

d) Imagine a world that was all black and white. How would it be different to ours? Would you prefer to live there or here?

e) Imagine a world where everyone could choose exactly what they looked like and also change what they looked like from week to week. What would it be like? How would it be different to ours? Would you rather live there or here?

f)   Imagine a world where everyone remembered everything they were ever told and everything they ever read. How would it be different to ours? Would you prefer to live there or here?

g)   Imagine a world where everyone could pop back and forwards in time for up to a week. What would this world be like? How would it be different to ours? Would you prefer to live there or here?

h)   Imagine a world in which everyone could stop time for as long as they liked and live in the gaps whilst everyone else was frozen. What would it be like? How would it be different to ours? Would you rather live there or here?

i)   Imagine a world where you had unlimited money. What would you do? Would you be happy?

j)   Imagine a world in which you could reassemble the atoms in things and change them into other things (eg your table into a hamburger, a missile into a flower). Everyone else could do this too. What would it be like? Would you rather live here or there? (Note: nanotechnology means that this world may exist in the future).

BIG IDEA 35:
Invention and discovery

a) What is the difference between an invention and discovery?

b) When Apple made the iPad were they inventing something new, or where they just combining a laptop and an iPhone?

c) Were cars invented or was the 'first' car just an assembly of a lot of smaller inventions to do with engines, wheels etc?

d) Imagine we invent an intergalactic spaceship in the next thousand years, and then travel to another galaxy. There we meet a species who invented intergalactic spaceships millions of years ago. Have we really invented the intergalactic spaceship?

e) Kentucky Fried Chicken (KFC) is made (apparently) with the Colonel's 12 secret herbs and spices. Was this combination sitting around in the universe waiting to be discovered or did the Colonel invent this recipe from nothing?

f) If everyone in the world was deaf, and then one person artificially created an ear that allowed people to hear, would she have 'invented' hearing for these people?

P.S.

Intuitionism is a mathematical philosophy founded by LEJ Brouwer (1881–1966) which says that maths itself is something created by human beings — ie invented. Intuitionists believe that there are no fundamental principles (such as addition) already existing in the world waiting to be discovered.

Plato (428BC–347 BC), on the other hand, believed that mathematical principles did exist in the world before people found them — ie they were *discovered*. Indeed, he believed that they existed in an abstract 'Realm of Forms' and that we detected them with our minds.

More conversation

a) When the first people started counting did they invent numbers or discover them?

b) Would 2+2 still equal 4 if nobody in the world could count?

c) Was mathematics an invention of people or is it a discovery about the nature of the world? If it is a discovery, where was it before people found it?

d) Are the following things inventions or discoveries?

    i.   cities

    ii. thoughts

    iii. dreams

    iv. time

    v. clocks

    vi. music

    vii. Beethoven's *Fifth Symphony*

BIG IDEA 36:
Science — good or bad
and paradigm shifts

BACKGROUND BRIEFING

Science is the act of finding out about the physical world (and the universe) through observing it and doing tests on it. Scientists use 'the scientific method' to make predictions, do experiments, get results and draw conclusions. In Ancient Greece it used to be called 'natural philosophy' but as a separate branch of study it has only flourished during the last few centuries.

a) What are some of the good things that science has brought us? (think electricity etc)

b) What are some of the bad things that science has brought us? (think weapons etc)

d) Do you think that science has brought the world more good things or bad?

e) If your religion told you one thing about the universe (eg that it is all the dream of the great god Brahma) and science told you another thing about the universe (eg it was created 13.9 billion years ago in the Big Bang) what should you do about this? Should you believe one or the other? Is there a way of believing both?

f) If science tells you something about the world that you may not like (eg that humans come from monkeys) do you have to believe it anyway?

g) If scientists developed a cure for all diseases would this be a good thing?

P.S.

It is possible distinguish between science (the discovery of the world) and technology (putting these discoveries into practice by making inventions).

Thomas Kuhn wrote about 'paradigm shifts' in a book called *The Structure of Scientific Revolutions*. In it he said that science goes down one track for a while until difficulties and problems mount up. Then a revolution in thinking occurs in which most of the old ideas are thrown out and replaced with new ones. These new ideas continue for a while until they are eventually replaced by another new revolution. This book made people think less about science as a single 'truth' and more about persuasive ways of thinking that improve on each other. Examples of paradigm shifts include the theory of evolution and the study of particles smaller than atoms (quantum mechanics).

More conversation

a) Can you think of any other paradigm shifts? Can you think of paradigm shifts in ways of thinking in general life? Have you had any paradigm shifts in the way you have thought about things?

b) If science is all about paradigm shifts, is it still true?

c) What is the difference between a science teacher and an English teacher? A science teacher and a religious studies teacher? A science teacher and a drama teacher?

BIG IDEA 37:
Design a different family

BACKGROUND BRIEFING

At the moment families often consist of one or two adults with a number of children. These children are usually the children of those adults. This is the 'nuclear family'. However, it is easy to imagine lots of different ways of society expecting family norms. They make us reflect on structures that we take for granted.

Conversation

a) Imagine a system where eight adults all get together to live. They all have children with each other in a compound of houses so that there would be eight adults and about 20 children in the average family compound. Would you like to live in such a set-up? What would be good and bad about it?

b) Imagine a system where partners were together, but all of the aunts, uncles, second cousins, third cousins etc all lived in a tribal group. Your aunts, uncles, older cousins etc all took care of you almost as much as your own parents. Would you like to live in such a set up? What would be good and bad about it?

c) Imagine the 'tribal' group above, except that nobody told you who your biological parents were. Instead you were told you had 10 or 15 'parents' who all loved you equally. Would you like to live in such a set up? What would be good and bad about it?

d) Imagine a society where groups of several hundred people would all live together in communities with long common dining tables, dormitories for children (looked after by matrons) etc. Would you like to live in such a set up? What would be good and bad about it?

e) Imagine a society where the government decided they wanted to give every child an 'equal opportunity'. So every child left their parents at the age of six and went to live in small boarding houses run by house staff. Children only saw their parents a few times a year. Would you like to live in such a society? Why or why not.

f) Imagine a society where one or two parents lived with their own children, but no-one else. Everything (meals, homework, sleeping) was based on that one nuclear family. Would you like to live in such a society? What would be good or bad about it?

P.S.

Other societies in history have not lived in the traditional nuclear family. Ancient Sparta was a society similar to conversation (e) above, where men and women did not live together and children were taken to strict boarding houses at the age of seven. They endured strict discipline and physical punishments to harden them.

(This society also had soldiers visit the mother at birth to check that the baby was strong — if it wasn't they took the baby away and left it on a hilltop to die.)

Tribal societies in Indigenous Australia and many parts of Africa had a complex kinship system similar to conversation (b) above. Bands of 10 or 20 people in a family grouping could join together into a tribe of several hundred for hunting and ceremonial purposes. There could also be clans of about 50 people. The kinship system in Indigenous Australia can allow for the naming of up to 70 different relations which far more than the number of European aunt/uncle/cousin terms.

BIG IDEA 38:
Design your own school

BACKGROUND BRIEFING

Just imagine that you have been put in charge of all of the schools in your country. You can make whatever changes you like and make them work straight away.

Make up your own schools. Some of the ideas below might help you along, or you may just design your own school from scratch.

Conversation

a) How much or how little would you use IT and computers in your school? What would you use them to do?

b) Could you use teaching videos on YouTube from the best teachers in the world to replace your teachers? Why/why not?

c) Could you use IT to connect with classrooms on the other side of the world? Could you have a classroom that was half in America and half in Australia? How?

d) Would you make the day longer or shorter? Would you have

a morning shift for some students and an afternoon shift for others?

e) How many lessons would there be and how much recess/lunchtime?

f) What would your classrooms look like? Would you have classrooms?

g) Could you have everyone learning from home using Skype or a similar programme to connect with each other?

h) Would you teach maths, English, science, history, geography and physical education? Would you teach more of some of them or less? Why?

i) Some schools have subjects like 'How we express ourselves' 'How we organise ourselves' and 'How we share the planet' instead of English/maths/science. Does this sound like a good idea?

j) Should there be lots of boarding schools that are log cabins in the countryside? You could go to these schools for five days a week and then just come home for the weekend.

k) Should everyone have to do sport, music, drama or a second language?

l) Should anyone be forced to do anything? Or should you just be able to come into the class when you felt like it?

m) Should children who are better at subjects be placed in the same class? Should students who are less good at subjects be placed in the same class? Why?

n) Do we need schools? Should children just go off to work and get training on the job?

BIG IDEA 39:
Punishing people

Conversation

Jasmin has had a terrible time at school. The 14-year old used to be average, but ever since the day her father fell down a well and didn't come out, she has been almost impossible to teach. She runs away from school to hang out at the shops and smokes at the school gates. When she is in a class she just talks, plays with her phone and swears at any teacher who tries to make her work. Today when a teacher asked her to do some maths she picked up a chair and threw it at her.

a) What do you think the school should do Jasmin? Why?
b) Should the school expel or suspend her?
   i.   What will happen to Jasmin then?
   ii. What will happen to the other people in the class if the school doesn't do this?
c) Should the school stop her from going to maths classes? Why/why not?
d) Should the school send her to the counsellor to work out

what has been going on with her father?

e) Should the maths teacher go to the police?

Conversation

Mark has had a terrible time at work. Five years ago he used to get into fights and was arrested. His boss has been saying how terrible his work is and making him feel awful. Last month his boss took $100 from his wages, saying that anyone who worked as badly as Mark did didn't deserve money, although Mark worked quite hard. Last week Mark went into his boss' office, picked up a chair and beat him with it. The boss has concussion and two broken arms. Yesterday Mark went to court and the judge sent him to gaol for six months.

a) Why would the judge send Mark to gaol? What purpose does it achieve?

b) Do you think Mark is less likely to be violent again if he goes to gaol?

c) Are there other things Mark will learn while he is in gaol?

d) Is the community safer now that Mark is in gaol for six months?

e) If Mark didn't go to gaol, do you think other people are more likely to beat their boss with a chair when they are frustrated? Why/why not?

P.S.

Some of the reasons that society punishes people are:

RETRIBUTION: This is similar to revenge — 'an eye for an eye' or 'atonement' — to give something back to the victim. It is a way that society shows that acts offend its shared sense of values.

DETERRENCE. The purpose of deterrence is to discourage people from committing the crime again in the future. The punishment (eg a prison sentence) may dissuade that individual from committing the crime again. It may also deter other people in society from committing a similar sort of crime in the future because other people see the consequence of the crime and decide not to try it.

REHABILITATION: The aim of rehabilitation is to change the mindset of the offender so that they realise that their act was wrong and they don't want to do it again.

PROTECTION: Society may imprison a person simply to protect the community. It may be unsafe for the society to have particularly violent people walking the streets with other people.

These purposes often work against each other eg rehabilitation would suggest shorter sentences, but general deterrence or retribution would suggest longer sentences.

More conversation
Jasmin, from the story above, didn't get over her father falling down a well and never being seen again. After being excluded from school she became a drug addict. She stole from houses and shops each day to feed her habit. One day whilst on the drug 'ice' she beat up a Charlie on the street to get his wallet. He is left with broken ribs and arms and becomes too afraid to leave his house.

a) If you are the judge, what would you do with Jasmin now?

b) Look at deterrence, rehabilitation, protection and retribution. How much would each of these figure in your sentence?

c) What chance do you think Jasmin has of living a normal life after some gaol time? Should we give her the chance?

If Jasmin could take a medicine every day that guaranteed she would never be violent again and also hate the idea of crime, would you let her take it? Would you then let her off going to gaol straight away? Why/why not?

BIG IDEA 40:
In gaol?

BACKGROUND BRIEFING

Imagine that you are the governor of a prison. In the prison are thieves, muggers, white collar criminals and the occasional murderer. They are in gaol from anything from a year to life. You get to design a brand new prison.

Conversation

a) Do you make each new 'cell' more like a prison cell or more like a bedroom?

b) Do you give the prisoners access to television? Cable TV? Foxtel? iTunes?

c) What sort of food do you provide every day?

d) Do you create a library for prisoners to borrow books?

e) Do you let them mingle or do you keep each prisoner in his or her own cell for almost all of the day?

f) Do you make each cell like a small dark hole with absolutely nothing to do?

g) Do you have cameras everywhere recording what the prisoners are doing? Does this include in the bathroom and the toilet?

h) Should the prison guards be polite or rude?

i) Do you make life a little easier for the people who have short sentences? Or do you make it easier for people who will never get out?

j) Is depriving people of their liberty (ie locking them up so they cannot wander around society) bad enough? Or should the conditions in the prison be terrible as well?

BIG IDEA 41:
Media

a) Imagine a society in which there were simply no newspapers, news shows or internet at all.

    a. How would it be different to ours?

    b. How would people find out what was happening in their country?

    c. *Would* people find out what was happening in their country?

    d. Could this society be fair?

b) Imagine a society where one person (let's call him Fergus Brown) owned most of the newspapers and news shows.

    a. If Fergus Brown believed that the earth was cooling down and got all of his newspapers to report that the Earth was cooling down, do you think that most people would end up believing that the Earth was cooling down?

    b. If Fergus Brown stopped printing news and only wrote stories about pop stars, celebrities and soap operas, would people become less intelligent?

    c. If Fergus Brown decided that he hated the Republican Presidential Candidate and loved the Democrat Presidential candidate in the US, could he persuade people to vote Democrat? Or not?

    d. If Fergus Brown decided to run for government himself, would he get in? How/why?

    e. Is Fergus Brown more powerful than the President?

c) Should the government own the newspapers? Why/why not?

d) In every city, should different people own all of the different newspapers? What would happen when there is only one newspaper in a city?

e) Imagine that a reporter for the newspaper has a bank robber admit to them that he robbed a bank. The robber also tells the journalist that he found out that the bank had been stealing its customers' money for years. The journalist reports this. The police ask the journalist for the name of the bank robber and she refuses to give it to them. They threaten to throw the journalist in goal.

    a. Should the journalist protect the bank robber's identity? Why/why not?

    b. Should the journalist go to gaol if she does not give up the name?

    c. What is the worse crime — the bank taking money out of each person's account, or the bank robber stealing money from the vault?

f) A journalist suspects that a businessman is actually a crook who cheats his customers. To find out more information should the journalist:

    a. pretend to be a customer?

b. pretend to interview the businessman about something easy, but then ask tough questions about cheating customers halfway through?

c. go through the businessman's garbage bins?

d. bug the businessman's house and hack his email?

e. make 'friends' with the businessman's wife and get her to admit things about her husband?

BIG IDEA 42:
The meaning of life

a) What is the meaning of life? (seriously)

b) Do dogs have a meaning of life? Or monkeys, whales or ants?

c) What would happen if there was no meaning to life? (eg to society, to your family etc)

d) Some people have suggested that the meaning of life is:

    a. to love and serve a God

    b. to be happy and/or to get pleasure

    c. to get as much as you can — eg to be rich and/or powerful

    d. to help other people — eg to do good

    e. to live out your own dreams — eg to be the best version of yourself

    f. to do something to further the human race

    g. to gain knowledge or wisdom

    h. non-existent (ie there is no meaning of life)

    i. to look for the meaning of life

What do you think of each of these as possible meanings of life?

Can you have more than one or two?

e) Why do you think many people try to ignore the meaning of life?

f) Why do people look for the meaning of life at all?

P.S.

Plato thought that the meaning of life was to gain the highest form of knowledge, and in doing so get yourself just a little closer to an 'ideal' form of good (see Plato).

Aristotle thought that the meaning of life was to be virtuous and strive for the highest form of good. If you did this you should achieve what he called 'Eudamonia' which is a complete form of sophisticated happiness.

Jesus Christ states that the meaning of life is to love and serve God, and to do to other people what you would hope they would do to you.

Buddha holds that the meaning of life is to end suffering. You do this by freeing yourself from attachment to things (eg wealth, property, people) because they cause unhappiness.

Immanuel Kant considered that the meaning of life lay in duty. He outlined what he called the 'categorical imperative'. This means that you check to see if an act is 'good' by asking 'what would happen if everyone did it' (eg steal/lie/give to charity).

Albert Camus was a 'nihilist' who thought that there was no meaning in life, and that the best that you could do was to live with some dignity in the face of an absurd universe.

Conversation

a) What do you think of the philosophers and religious figures above? Which ones help you the most?

b) Could famous philosophers/rulers/actors have had more meaning in their lives than average people because they affect so many millions of people?

c) What is the meaning of the word 'meaning'? What if our language has tricked us into thinking there is a meaning by inventing the word 'meaning'? (If this question is too hard, ignore it).

d) If there are no objective values that people can agree on, does this make life meaningless? Or not?

e) If it turned out that you were immortal would this make your life on earth less meaningful? Or more meaningful?

f) When most of these philosophies were written, the philosophers thought that there were just a few planets in existence Now we know that there are a hundred million galaxies each with hundreds of millions of stars. Does the size of the universe change the meaning of our lives? Or not? Why?

g) Douglas Adams wrote a book called *The Hitch-hikers Guide to the Galaxy* in which the meaning of life was (famously) 'Forty two'. Why do you think he did this? What was he trying to say about the meaning of life?

h) If you can work out a meaning of life that is good for you, is this enough? Does it matter if other people do not share it?

BIG IDEA 43:
More about dreams

a) What is a great dream that you have had (that you can discuss)? What is a bad nightmare?

b) What is different about a dream and real life? How can you tell the difference during the day? Can you tell the difference when you are in the middle of the dream?

c) Are the emotions you have in a nightmare (happiness/fear etc) *real* emotions?

d) Are the thoughts and ideas you have in dreams real thoughts and ideas?

e) What are the differences between thoughts and emotions you have in dreams and the ones you have when you are awake?

f) When you have a nightmare, should you be able to take the next day off school?

g) If you have a vivid dream about flying in a hot air balloon, have you actually had this experience?

h) Are our dreams a whole other life?

i) Can you learn anything from your dreams? If so what? (eg could you learn bravery by being brave in a dream?)

j)   Imagine that you have a dream about being chased by ninja assassins, and then you wake up in your bed. You lie in a sweat in your sheets, relieved that it was just a dream. Then ninja assassins start climbing through your window and you have to flee. Then you wake up 'again' and lie sweating in your bed — you realise that the last time you 'woke up' it was all just part of a dream. How can you know that you have really woken up from your dream this time?

P.S.

The philosopher Wittgenstein held that you could not really ask the question 'Am I dreaming' whilst you were in the middle of a dream. This is because when you are dreaming, the words 'Am I dreaming' are also a part of the dream. The idea that the words 'I' 'am' and 'dreaming' have any meaning at all are also part of the dream.

More conversation

a) Can you think 'I am dreaming' in the middle of a dream? Is it a real thought?

b) If you dream that 2+2=5 in the dream, is this *true* for the world of your dream?

c) Are any thoughts in your dream real?

d) Are the other people in your dream real?

e) Could we be the products of someone else's dream right now? Why/why not?

f)   Some Hindus believe that we are all the dream of the great God Brahma. What do you think of this idea?

BIG IDEA 44:
Dreams of power

a) Imagine you could become the Prince or Princess of England. You could spend your life in palaces, going to parties and touring the world. Think of the downside: what about the media attention or having your role defined your whole life? Would you do it?

b) Imagine that you become the ruler of the world. You have all the power to do exactly what you want with and to anyone you want. Think of the downside: what sort of person might you be after 20 years of this? Would you do it?

c) Imagine that you become the President of the US. You have power, influence, prestige and the ability to make a big difference. Think of the downside: what about your safety, what about your family? Would you do it?

d) Imagine that you become a teen idol. Your album is at Number One, your concerts are sell-outs and calendars of you are on every teenage girl/boy's wall. Think of the downside: what about the publicity, the dangers of celebrity and the lures of easy fame? Would you do it?

e) Imagine that you win the lottery and have two hundred million dollars delivered to your door — money, money money. Guess what... there may still be a downside. Would your family survive the change, what sort of people would you become, who would your friends be, would your 'friends' just want you for your money? Would you do it?

BIG IDEA 45: More when do you stop being you?

a) If your favourite food changed from ice-cream to sushi, would you still be you?

b) If you had all of your memories wiped and then replaced with all of the memories, personality etc of another person called Chris, would you still be you? Why?

c) If you suddenly hated all of your favourite foods and liked every food you used to hate, would you still be you?

d) If you started losing your memories, so that you thought that the woman down the street was your mother and the boy at the newsagent was your brother, would you still be you?

e) If a brick fell on your head and your personality changed so that you were much more angry, frustrated and negative than you are now, would you still be you? Why?

f) If a second passes and you have a new thought, are you still you?

g) If you have a sleeping dream that you are a warrior fighting dinosaurs. *At that moment*, are you still you?

h) Imagine that between the ages of eight and ten you fell into a deep sleep from which no-one can wake you. You then wake up. Years later, scientists replace the 'lost' two years with memories of you taking a wonderful trip around the world. These memories feel incredibly real. Would you still be you?

i) What is you? What makes you you from one year to the next?

BIG IDEA 46:
Gaia

BACKGROUND BRIEFING

In 1965 the scientist James Lovelock was working at NASA on the space programme trying to see if there was life on Mars. NASA scientists had decided that a way of spotting if something was living was that it 'reduced entropy', which means that it made its own environments more ordered (eg a room left on its own gets messy and dusty, but living people come and clean it up). Mars and Venus seemed dead, but he found that the whole of Earth's environment seemed incredibly complicated. It also seemed very well set up for life. For example he found that the overall average temperature on Earth has stayed at 15°C — perfect for life — for hundreds of millions of years, even though the amount of light from the sun has changed over this time. This got James Lovelock wondering about the nature of the Earth.

Conversation

a) If there were two thinking blood cells inside your body, do you think they would work out that they were living inside a giant body? Or would they not believe it?

b) Coral in a reef is alive. Is the coral reef 'alive'?

c) Could the whole surface of the Earth be 'alive'? If so, what are all the parts of its 'body?' How does it work?

d) How do you usually tell if something is alive? How is the Earth similar to this? How is it different to this?

e) Can something be alive without thinking? Can the Earth be alive without thinking?

P.S.

James Lovelock went on in 1979 to write the book *Gaia: A New Look at Life on Earth*. He suggested that it is incredibly unlikely that the conditions for life could exist on Earth and also stay that way for so long — we are like a Garden of Eden in a space desert. He said that the Earth itself regulates the environment to keep it so perfect for living creatures. It makes sure all of the pieces of nature work together in one big whole. This means 'we may find ourselves and all other living things to be part and partners of a vast being who in her entirety has the power to maintain our planet as a fit and comfortable habitat for life.' He called this being 'Gaia'.

More conversation

a) What do you think of James Lovelock's idea?

b) Is it going too far to say that just because an environment keeps itself 'fresh' that it is alive? (Could 'Gaia' just be a simile?)

c) SOME SCIENTISTS SAY THAT EVOLUTION IS NOT ENOUGH TO EXPLAIN WHY ALL THE PIECES OF THE ENVIRONMENT FIT TOGETHER SO NEATLY.

(Note: the majority don't say this.) What do you think of this view?

d) When trying to study something (eg the climate) should you break the study up into smaller and smaller parts, or should you try to put everything together into one big picture? What are the disadvantages of each method?

e) Imagine that the Earth was alive and thinking. What would it think of people?

f) If Gaia exists, are we a part of it? Or do we live on it?

g) In 2009, James Lovelock went on to say that human beings are an infection on the planet. Why would he say this? What do you think of this view?

BIG IDEA 47:
Chaos (harder one)

BACKGROUND BRIEFING

In 1961 the meteorologist Edward Lorenz was running a computer simulation about the weather. To take a short cut he rounded out some of the decimals in the numbers by a tiny percentage — one in a thousand (eg there is almost no difference between 24.1°C and 24.2°C). He thought this would make no difference to the weather predictions. Instead it made all the difference in the world. The weather pattern that the computer created was completely different to the simulation before it. This got Lorenz thinking.

Conversation

a) Can you predict anything? Can you predict anything accurately?

b) If you created a computer powerful enough do you think you could put in all of the data about what the world was like right now and predict what it was going to be like in the future?

(Centuries-old scientists such as Pierre Laplace and Isaac Newton thought that you could.)

P.S.

Edward Lorenz came up with the idea that weather and many other physical systems were *chaotic*, that is, not predictable at all. He went on to write a paper called 'Does the Flap of a Butterfly's Wings in Brazil set off a Tornado in Texas'? In this paper he suggested that small differences at the start can lead to huge differences later on.

More conversation

a) Do you think the flap of a butterfly's wings could really cause a tornado? How?

b) Could the flap of a million butterfly's wings, and about a billion other factors, all cause a tornado?

c) Do you think it is possible to predict the weather very far into the future?

d) Do you think this means that the world works randomly from day to day?

e) Can 'the butterfly effect' work in other aspects of life as well? Can small decisions you make lead to giant effects later on? What would be an example of this in your own life?

f) Can we predict the way our lives will unfold?

BIG IDEA 48: Infinity and space

BACKGROUND BRIEFING

Something is infinite if it is without any end, boundary or limit. It is just about impossible to properly imagine, but it can give your mind a stretch trying. The term was first used mathematically, that we know of, by Zeno of Elea (who also wrote the paradoxes in Big Idea 12). Indian philosophers have broken up infinity into the two categories: 'countless' (eg numbers) and 'endless' (eg space).

a) How big can a number be? Is there any such thing as the largest number, or can there always be a bigger one?

b) If you wrote a number on a piece of paper that started with a 1 and then had so many zeroes in it that the paper it was written on filled up the whole galaxy, would this number be as big as infinity? Would it be tiny compared to infinity?

c) Are some infinities bigger than others? For example is the infinite amount of numbers between 1 and 5 bigger than the infinite amount of numbers between 1 and 2?

d) Is the universe infinite or does it stop somewhere?

e) If the universe stops somewhere, what is beyond that? Isn't that just more universe?

f) If the universe goes on forever, that means that every combination of atoms has happened... and happened infinite times. This means that there are many (indeed and infinite) number of 'yous' around the universe all doing different things as we speak. Is this possible?

P.S. (HARDER)

Albert Einstein got around the idea of an infinite universe by saying that space is *curved*. We know of three dimensions in space: length, breadth and height. He said there was *fourth* too. This fourth dimension is curved so that the whole universe is like a giant four-dimensional sphere that you could keep going around and around. So the universe is 'finite but unbounded'.

A question that arises is that if the universe is a four-dimensional sphere, then what is outside that sphere? Einstein would say that this question makes no sense. Instead, you should imagine that the universe is a cake. Dimensions of space are *ingredients* of the cake. The ingredients have been tipped into a cake bowl. Asking what is outside the universe is like asking what ingredients of the cake are outside the cake. There are none because all of the ingredients of a cake are *in* the cake.

More conversation

a) Imagine creatures that are only have two dimensions: length and breadth. What would they think if they met you — a creature with length, breadth and height? How would they see you?

b) Imagine that you met a creature that 'existed' in four spatial dimensions (length, breadth, height and something else). Can you imagine this at all?

c) Imagine you are travelling through the universe with Einstein. What happens eventually? Do you:

    a. just keep going forever?

    b. turn up back where you started?

    c. hit the edge of the 'cake' universe?

    d. something else?

Einstein's ideas about space have been proved many times. Nonetheless, it is hard to get your head around. Is it possible to accept something without fully being able to understand it?

Universal musings

    a) Could our universe be part of a much larger universe?

    b) Could there be thousands of different universes out there?

    c) Could each of our atoms on our body be a universe?

    d) Could our universe be an atom in a much grander body?

    e) Could our universe be a computer programme?

    f) When we dream, is that a universe for the creatures in our dream?

    g) Could our universe be the dream of a creature?

BIG IDEA 49:
Time (harder)

Conversation

a) How long does it take to travel 100 metres? How long does it take to travel 100 seconds?

b) Can time slow down or speed up, even when we are in the middle of it? How would we know?

c) Does time travel more slowly when you are bored?

d) Is there any way at all of measuring the speed of time?

e) Stop. Close your eyes. See if you can *feel* time passing. What does it feel like?

f) If you could go backwards in time, where would you go? What would you do?

g) If you could go forwards in time, where would you go? What would you do?

P.S.

In 1905, Einstein discovered that time is not the stately unchangeable phenomena that everyone had previously assumed it was. Instead time is just another dimension, like length, breadth and height. A major difference is that we are 'trapped' inside the dimension of time and can't move around it in the same way that we can move around a park (length and breadth) or go up and down an escalator (height). However, time speeds up for you (just a bit) when you move and time speeds up (just a bit) when there is more and more gravity.

a) How can time be a 'dimension'? Why does this sound bizarre?

b) Can there be things that are real (eg time) yet beyond our own capacity to imagine them?

c) If 'time' is a dimension, could there be other dimensions too? Can you possibly think of some other ones?

d) Could time be like a river? Does it flow from the past to the future?

e) Could time be like the light of a torch travelling along a rug/carpet? All of the past, present and future are already there (like the patterns in the rug), but the moving light of the torch only lights up one bit of the rug at a time.

   a. If the past, present and future are all already there (like the pattern on the rug/carpet) does this mean that your future is set?

BIG IDEA 50:
Circus act 1 — The mind swap

BACKGROUND BRIEFING

Imagine two boys, Bob and Ferdinand, who each go to the circus and visit 'The Amazing Mephisto's' booth. The Amazing Mephisto offers them 'The Swap of a Lifetime' — sight unseen. They agree. Each of them walks into a darkened booth. On the other side they can just see about 20 people in an audience watching. Each of them feels something tingly and strange on the top of their heads.

The audience gasps. The Great Mephisto is draining each of their minds. Everything in each of their minds is trickling into two bottles.

Then the audience gasps again because the Great Mephisto has now swapped the bottles and is pouring the thoughts back into the boys' heads! However, she is pouring Bob's mind into Ferdinand's body and Ferdinand's mind into Bob's body!!

Each head blinks. Each body starts to move. Who is who?

Person 1	Person 2
(Ben's body, Ferdinand's mind)	(Ferdinand's body, Ben's mind)

Conversation

a) The Great Mephisto knows that Ben loved sushi before and Ferdinand hated it. He offers them both some sushi. Who takes it, Person 1 or Person 2?

b) The Great Mephisto knows that Ferdinand was a great runner and Ben was terrible. He makes them run a race. Who wins, Person 1 or Person 2?

c) The Great Mephisto knows that Ben was excellent at maths problems and Ferdinand was terrible. He sets them both a maths quiz. Who wins it, Person 1 or Person 2?

d) The Great Mephisto gets each of them to go to their mothers. Who goes to who?

e) When Person 1 has a new thought, whose thought is it? Is it a Ben thought or a Ferdinand thought?

f) Who is who? Is there a Ben in a Ferdinand body, or are there two entirely new people at the circus?

BIG IDEA 51: Circus act 2 — The transporter

BACKGROUND BRIEFING

You go to the circus. Down one garish lane you see two booths on opposite sides of the street, on each the writing says: 'Come inside and be transported!' Curious, you go into one of them. The booth owner, dressed in bizarre circus gear, gets you to step inside a metal box. He closes the door around you, and you feel as if there is a light around your head — as if something is scanning your every thought. Suddenly, BANG, you are in another box. You step out and you are on the other side of the street in the other booth.

Another man, also in bizarre circus gear, leads you out of the box. Amazed, you ask what has happened. The man explains that every one of your thoughts and memories were scanned and downloaded by a superpowerful computer. At the same time it scanned the position of every one of your atoms. All of this information was sent to another supercomputer across the road.

Then in one moment, your body and brain were disassembled in one booth and reassembled in the other. Each booth is joined up to a vat of atoms (like Lego blocks) so the booth had all the materials and information it needed to recreate you with the information. You are a bit stunned. You look across the road and see the booth you first went into where the first circus man is waving smugly.

Conversation

a) Is the person who stepped out of the second booth you?

b) Have you actually been killed, and this 'you' is now just a copy of you with the same memories?

c) If a computer has scanned all of your memories, thoughts, brain positions and atoms, has it scanned all of you?

d) If there was an half-hour delay between disassembling you and reassembling you, where were you for this time?

e) Imagine that there is a malfunction in the second booth. After you step out of the machine it whirrs again. A minute later *another* 'you' steps out of the machine. Is this version you too? Or are you the real you? What if this other person is convinced they are you too?

f) What if all of the information about you is sent to a clothing factory in China, and the owner uses the information to create one thousand 'yous' to work on the clothing production line. Are all of these people you?

    a. If all of these people escaped and went to your home, how crowded would your house become? Would every one of the thousand people be delighted so see their very own mum and/or dad? What would your parents do?

    b. Do you think you would all get on? Would you fight? If 'you' were one of these thousand people, would you be any more genuine that the other 999 'yous'?

BIG IDEA 52: Philosopher(s) 1 — Wise early men of Greece

BACKGROUND BRIEFING

From where we stand at the beginning of the twenty-first century, the ideas of some of the first Ancient Greek philosophers can seem simple, wrong and quaint. However, we need to remember that these philosophers were starting to use reason from scratch — they had no-one's shoulders to stand on when they considered the biggest questions in the world.

Imagine that we travel in a time machine back to Ancient Greece, armed with all of our knowledge of the world. We go to the marketplace of Athens, where there just happens to be a philosophy conference on. The two questions for the conference are:

i. How do things change from one thing to another (eg from non-living to living)?

ii. What is the basic substance at the root of all change?

Philosophers from everywhere have come to share ideas and word quickly gets around that you are the wisest and the most knowing philosopher of all. However, you are not going to be a smartypants and tell them all your twenty-first century knowledge straight out. Instead you are first going to listen to each philosopher's ideas seriously, before helping them out.

Conversation

a) Thales runs up to you and says 'I know, I know what the basic substance is. It is WATER. Because water is everywhere an in everything'. What do you say to help Thales? (apart from saying 'No'.)

b) Anaximanes rushes up to you and pushes Thales aside. 'No, no,' he says. 'The most basic substance is air and vapour! Water is just condensed air. And air is all around us.' What do you say to help Anaximanes?

c) Parmenides strides up to you knowingly. 'Nothing can ever change' he says. 'It stands to reason that one thing cannot turn into another.' You tell him that we can *see* things changing all the time. 'Ahh yes,' said Parmenides. 'I know, I know. My reason tells me that things cannot change and my senses tell me that they are changing. But our senses can deceive us. We should always believe our reason over our senses.' What do you say to help Parmenides?

d) Heraclitus runs up to you and Parmenides glares at him. 'Don't listen to Parmenides' says Heraclitus. 'Actually, everything is in a constant state of flux — rivers, atmosphere, even people. Nothing ever stays the same and nothing happens twice.' What do you say to help Heraclitus?

e) Empedocles strolls over and says 'Oh dear, are those two fighting again? Look, I think they are actually both right in one way. Parmenides is right when he says that things don't change. And Heraclitus is right when he says that everything appears to change. What is actually happening is that unchanging small pieces are mixing together and separating, giving the appearance of change (a bit like a painter mixing colours). There are four roots — earth, air, fire and water.' What do you say to Empedocles?

f) Democritus then barrels into all of you. 'I have it, I have it!' he says. 'I think I know what is at the base of things. Atoms... Atoms [this is 500BC remember]. These atoms are the smallest piece of matter, they can't be cut and they are eternal too. The universe is actually all changing pieces of atoms. The soul too is atoms. Even though it feels different, it is made up of special soul atoms that fly apart when people die and re-join as new people.' You are a little taken aback (after all there are no electron microscopes in Ancient Greece). What do you say to Democritus?

g) Socrates then strides up. You have a sense that he is very famous indeed. He says 'The way to work out what is right and wrong is for people to use their own reason and thinking. All ideas have to be chewed over in conversation with people agreeing and disagreeing with each other. It is by conversing, disagreeing and building on each other's ideas that we will come to the best ideas. In fact, this is such a good idea that the world will come to call it 'The Socratic Method'. What do you say to Socrates? Should you get him to come and talk to your teachers?

BIG IDEA 53:
Philosopher 2 — Plato

BACKGROUND BRIEFING

Plato lived from 428–347 BC. His philosophy has been incredibly influential through Western thought and Christianity. He was particularly interested in ideas and where they came from.

Conversation

a) If you want to really know what the shape of the perfect homemade cup cake is like, should you go to an example of a very good cup cake, or should you go to the mould that made all of the different cupcakes? Why?

b) If you want to know what the perfect cow is like, should you go to an example of a very good cow, or should you imagine an ideal cow? Do you think that there could be an ideal cow, of which all real cows are just copies? What about an ideal cupboard or an ideal person?

c) We find out some things using our 'senses' (eg whether

a wheel in your car is a circle or flat). We find out some other things using our reason (eg a perfect circle always has 360°). Which is the better way of finding out about a circle?

d) Is there *any such thing* as a perfect circle in real life? Can we have the idea of a perfectly round circle in our minds?

e) Plato thought that there was realm called the 'world of ideas' or the 'realm of forms' that contains all of the perfect versions of things that exist in our world. What do you think of this idea?

f)   Plato thought that things in our world (the 'realm of becoming') were inferior versions of things in the 'realm of forms'. He thought this because everything in our world changes, dies or decomposes; even rocks eventually wear away. By contrast he thought that the perfection of the 'realm of forms' is unchanging. Do you agree that change makes our world imperfect?

P.S.

Plato explained his idea about a realm of forms by using a story about cave shadows (which is one of the most famous stories in all of philosophy). Imagine someone who has been tied up since birth in a cave with her head restrained so that she can only see the back wall of the cave. Behind her is a fire. People walk across the mouth of the cave and birds fly by but all the girl sees are the shadows of these things on the wall on the cave. She thinks the shadows are *all* of reality until one day when her ropes loosen and she frees herself. She turns around and suddenly she sees depth, colour, people and animals. She realises that all her life she had just been seeing shadows.

Plato says that we too are like creatures tied up in a cave. The animals, people and things that we see are just shadows of the 'real' versions. In contrast, ideas, reason and logic, which feel like shadows in our minds, are actually the most real things in this much greater realm of forms.

This belief in an eternal and unchanging perfect world of ideas (which is totally different from our ever-changing world of experience) is the basis of most of his philosophy.

More conversation

a) What do you think of Plato's cave shadows idea? Could ideas such as truth, beauty and mathematics really be just shadows of the real thing? And could those things really be the building blocks of a much greater world?

b) If several people were all tied up in the cave together and the girl went back to tell her friends what she had seen, would they believe her? Why/why not?

c) Do you think Plato is right to put such an emphasis on ideas instead of actual things that exist in the world (eg real cows, real people, real cupboards)?

d) Do you think there is a perfect 'justice' that we try to reach with all of our laws?

e) Did you ever feel a 'longing' to be a part of this world of ideas even before you knew what it was? Plato believes that every soul (eg your soul) comes from the world of forms and 'wakes up' in a body. When you see a real cow you faintly remember the ideal version back in the world of forms. Each of us develops a longing to return to the realm of forms — which is like being homesick for a home you can't remember. What do you think of this? Can you even *imagine* this realm of forms Plato says you come from? How?

f) Plato also speaks of the highest form of love being a divinely inspired love of intellectual beauty. This has come to be known as platonic love. What do you think of this idea?

g) Plato also imagined a perfect society:

    a. ruled by philosophers

    b. a place where rulers had to give away all their possessions and have no families (so that they could focus on ruling better)

    c. where women and men could equally rule

    d. where if you were born a slave you stayed a slave, if you were born a trader you stayed a trader and if you were born a ruler/philosopher you stayed this way too

    e. where children were raised by the state

h) What is good and what is bad about this system? Would you want to live in this system?

BIG IDEA 54:
Philosopher 3 —
Aristotle (on ideas)

Note: You should talk about Aristotle after Plato because much of what Aristotle says argues against Plato's statements.

BACKGROUND BRIEFING

Aristotle lived from 384–322BC and was the last of the extremely well known Ancient Greek philosophers. He was taught by Plato and he tutored Alexander the Great for three years before Alexander conquered most of the known world. Aristotle went on to found his own philosophy school, called the 'Lyceum'. Many of his ideas were almost the opposite of Plato's.

In particular, Aristotle held that we got the 'idea' of something (eg a cow) by looking at a lot of real cows and forming a collective idea in our head. The idea of 'cow' certainly didn't drift down from an abstract realm of forms, as Plato would have said. He believed we got ideas from our senses (eg sight, sound, touch, taste and smell). In other words we got ideas from the ground up, not the top down.

Conversation

a) Do you get your idea of a 'cow' by seeing a dozen real 'cows'?

b) Is there anything such thing as the 'idea' of a cow without real cows?

c) Aristotle thought that the 'idea' of a cow was present in every single cow — it was like a body and a soul mixed together. What do you think of this? How does it compare to Plato's ideas?

d) If there was no-one to think about cows, would there still be the 'idea' of a cow at all?

e) Did you get your idea of a circle by seeing real circles, or by thinking about the ideal circle (ie something with 360°).

P.S.

Aristotle thought that nothing at all could exist in our minds (or our consciousness) until our senses had first perceived it. Without our senses there was no consciousness at all. The thing that we do in our heads is 'organise' the information from our senses (eg so that 12 cows we see become the idea 'cow' and we don't mix a horse up in the middle).

More conversation

a) Do we get the idea of numbers and maths (eg 2+2=4) from seeing real objects lined up on the ground as Aristotle would say? Or do they come from an ideal 'realm' that we then apply to the real objects lying around on the ground, as Plato would say?

b) Could we have any ideas at all if we did not have any senses (ie no sight, smell, touch, hearing or taste)?

c) If *no-one* had any senses would there be any ideas at all in the world?

d) If there were no people at all would 2+2 still equal 4?

e) If there were not four things in the universe, could there still be the idea 2+2=4?

P.P.S.

Like Plato, Aristotle wrote about the best way to govern a society. He thought that a monarchy or kingship would be effective as long as it did not turn into a tyranny (ie where the king or queen rule only for themselves). The second was an aristocracy, in which there was a 'class' of people who ruled for the benefit of everyone. Again, if this wasn't done well it would turn into an oligarchy where a small number of rich people disregarded the needs of the poor. The third version was a 'polity' where everybody participates. This is similar to a democracy, which Aristotle worried could develop into a situation where the poor disregarded the needs of the rich. (In Aristotle's democracy however, citizens voted on each issue and magistrates were chosen randomly — so it was a much more extreme form of democracy than we know today.)

Even more conversation

a) What do you think of Aristotle's worries about democracy? Is this justified? Are there faults in democracy that you can see?

b) What do you think about Aristotle being comfortable with monarchies and aristocracies? Does this give us something to consider, or should we disregard his views as being too old fashioned?

BIG IDEA 55:
Philosopher 3 continued — Aristotle (on happiness and virtue)

BACKGROUND BRIEFING

Aristotle was hugely influential in two areas of ethical thought: how to be happy and how to live a good life.

Conversation

a) How much do each of the following things make you happy? (Rank them if you can OR play 'would you rather' for two of them at a time until you work out your favourite few).

    a. eating your favourite flavoured ice cream

    b. being able to vote when you are older

    c. watching movies

    d. playing a game of your favourite sport

e. knowing that you can travel wherever you want without soldiers shooting you

f. getting a good mark after studying hard

g. loving your dog/cat/bird/goldfish

h. having a fantastic conversation with a friend

i. knowing that there are police employed in your country to catch criminals who might otherwise hurt you

j. talking about ideas with anyone (eg your parents)

k. swimming in the waves

l. knowing that you are lucky to be safe and well fed when half the population of the earth is not safe or not well fed

m. the first sip of your favourite drink

n. knowing your parents love you

P.S.

Aristotle wrote about a very broad type of happiness he called 'eudamonia'. It actually meant more than happiness; it was more like 'well-being' or 'flourishing'. He thought that eudamonia should be the major reason why people did things. There were three types of activities that led to eudamonia and each was more important than the last. They were:

- pleasure
- life as a responsible citizen in a free state
- life as a thinker, particularly a philosophical thinker

a) How is eudamonia different from pleasure or happiness? If we live our lives seeking 'well-being' how would it be different from a life seeking pleasure or happiness?

b) Of the things above that make you happy, which ones could be called pleasure, which are examples of life as a responsible citizen and which are examples of life as a thinker? Which are none of these?

c) What things should make you happy? What things DO make you happy? Is there a way to get more happiness out of the things that SHOULD make you happy?

P.P.S.

Aristotle said that virtuous people lived a 'golden mean'. This means that in various areas of human behaviour they do not do too little nor too much. For example in the area of 'courage' they do not too little because that would be 'cowardly', nor do they do too much because that would be 'reckless'. Instead finding the middle ground means finding genuine courage. Aristotle's views about virtues have become much more well regarded in the last 50 years as part of an idea called 'virtue ethics'. Virtue ethics suggests you look at good people to work out what is ethical behaviour.

Even more conversation

a) What would be a 'golden mean' with regard to:
   a. saving and spending money?
   b. getting angry?
   c. knowing yourself (good and bad things)?

b) Do you think that a golden mean is a good way of thinking about living well? Or is all this talk of balance and well-being too average?

BIG IDEA 56:
Philosopher 4 –
Descartes

BACKGROUND BRIEFING

René Descartes was born in 1596 and died in 1650. During his life Descartes said he wanted to doubt everything and start philosophy again. He wanted to use only ideas that he could directly prove, instead of ideas that were handed down. However, it turned out that there was almost nothing he could rely on to prove things. For a start, he couldn't rely on his senses because senses can deceive us.

Conversation

a) Descartes thought that you can't use your senses to even prove you are awake. This is because you can believe you are awake while you are in the middle of a dream.

    a. Could you be in the middle of a dream right now? (see also

Big Idea 2: Are you in the middle of a dream?)

b. Could an evil demon be pumping thoughts into your head making you think you are sitting in a chair reading this book? Can you prove that this is not true?

b) Descartes thought there were two types of reason. One involved ideas with 'quantitative properties' (eg maths), which are purely mental, while others involved ideas with 'qualitative properties' (eg colour) which are less reliable because we gain them through our senses.

a. Is maths more reliable to you than colour or taste?

b. Which is more *real* to you? Which is more *important* to you?

P.S.

Descartes was left with very little he could rely on. However, he did realise that he could hear himself thinking and thus he could prove to himself he was existing. He may be thinking in a dream or he may be thinking the wrong thoughts, but he could still prove he was thinking. This led to his most famous single statement: 'I think therefore I am' (*Cogito Ergo Sum*).

a) Think the thought 'carrots' in your head. Do you hear a voice in your head? You can absolutely prove to yourself that you can hear it. You may not be able to prove carrots exist, but that's not the point. *You think, therefore you exist*. What do you think of this idea?

b) Can you prove to anyone else that you are thinking? How do *they* know you are not a very advanced robot, or a virtual reality simulation? Does it matter whether you can prove you are thinking to them?

c) Could there be thoughts floating around, under the *illusion* that there is someone thinking them (ie you) when there is not really? Could it be that there are just thoughts?

d) How are the physical and the non-physical parts of you connected?

   a. When you have sad feelings why does water start to come from your eyes?

   b. When you make a decision to move your leg forward, why does your leg move forward?

   c. When you have happy thoughts, why does your mouth turn upwards?

P.P.S.

Descartes said that his consciousness/thoughts and his body were two different types of substances (although the mind doesn't take up any space). This makes him a dualist. He also thought that mind and brain were linked by a gland called the pineal gland.

Descartes went on to say that the next thing he could imagine was the idea of perfection. If you can *imagine* a perfect thing, then a *real* version of it must exist. Therefore the perfect being exists.

e) Do you agree with Descartes that the mind and the body are completely separate types of substance?

f) What IS your consciousness if it is not matter?

g) What is *more* you, your consciousness or your body?

h) Does the pineal gland answer the problem of the mind/body split? Or not? (Of course later medical science has shown that there is not actually a gland with this function).

i) *Descartes believed that the body was an automaton, like a machine, powered by our thoughts.* Do you think that the mind controls the body, the body controls the mind, or neither?

j)   *Descartes believed that animals were all automatons and did not have minds to reason at all.* Do you agree with this part of his philosophy? Why/why not?

BIG IDEA 57:
Philosopher 5 — Locke

BACKGROUND BRIEFING

John Locke was an Englishman who was born in 1632 and died in 1704. He was very different from Descartes and Plato. Those philosophers thought that there were 'innate' ideas in the mind (eg maths) disconnected from your senses. Locke thought the opposite. He thought that everything *started* with the senses and that without your senses there were no ideas to have. This made him what was called an 'empiricist'. It also brought his philosophy closer to the ideas of Aristotle.

Conversation

a) Where do you think your ideas come from:
   a. the world?
   b. other ideas you have had?
   c. a mystical realm of ideas?
   d. somewhere else?

b) Locke thought that before we perceived things with our senses, our mind was like a whiteboard with nothing written on it. He called it 'tabula rasa', or 'blank slate'. Do you think our minds starts off as blank slates? Why/why not?

c) Locke thought that the role of the mind is to clarify, organise and process all of the things that we see, hear smell etc. He believed we started doing this as very young children by turning *sensation* of objects into *reflection* about them. Is this how your mind thinks? Or can your mind think about things other than the senses?

d) Can we rely on our senses? Are there some senses we can rely on more than others?

P.S.

Locke stated that there are two types of qualities to things in the world. You can rely on one and not the other.

The first are 'primary qualities': features such as number and weight. They are features of the object itself. You can rely on these.

The second are 'secondary qualities'. These are elements such as colour, taste and sound. These involve people's *perception* of an object. People experience these qualities differently and you cannot rely on these.

More conversation

a) What is the difference between thinking an apple is round and thinking an apple tastes good?

b) Is Locke right about primary qualities? Can you think of any times when you cannot rely on numbers (eg counting things) or weight (eg measuring weight in space)?

c) If you like a song and your friend hates it, have you heard the same song? Can you rely on your senses here? Have you:

    a. experienced sound differently?

    b. made different judgements about a sound you both heard the same way?

P.P.S.

John Locke also wrote about the idea of a social contract. He thought that when you chose to live in a state, you made a social contract with it to obey all of its laws. You couldn't just pick the laws you liked and obey only those. This may mean you have to obey laws you don't like. However, he also thought that there were some laws that were so unjust (today we would include 'slavery' and 'no votes for women' amongst them) that it would be okay — indeed a duty — not to obey them.

Even more conversation

a) Do you think that we need to obey laws we don't agree with (eg speeding limits, drugs, school rules)? Or can we just pick the rules we agree with?

b) Are there laws that we would be wrong to obey? Can you think of any examples? Do you think you would obey them anyway, or would you disobey them and risk trouble from the government and the police?

BIG IDEA 58: Philosopher 6 — Hume

BACKGROUND BRIEFING

David Hume (1711–1776) lived in both France and England. When his first attempts at philosophy failed he became, as Bertrand Russell says, 'tutor to a lunatic and then secretary to a general'. He followed on from Locke and went even further than Locke. In short, he took 'empiricism' (the idea that there was no separate ideas, but instead only what you could work out from your senses) to logical extremes. These extremes are very uncomfortable but sometimes hard to argue against.

Conversation

a) Imagine that you trip and knock your shin. What is stronger, the pain you feel at that moment or the idea/memory of the pain in the minutes and months to come? Is it the *sensation* or the *idea* of pain that is worse?

b) Hume says (like Locke) that all of your ideas are cutting and pasting the impressions you get. Do you agree? Do you think you have ideas that are NOT cutting and pasting your impressions?

c) Hume thought that ideas were very weak compared to impressions. He said 'by ideas I mean the faint images of these [impressions] in thinking and reasoning'. Do you agree with this?

d) Can you get a sensation of your own mind? If you can't, can you have an *idea* of your own mind? Can you know yourself?

P.S.

Hume was very taken with impressions. He thought that almost everything was the result of impressions that were connected. He didn't even believe that there was such a thing as an 'I' (ie you or anyone else). He thought that 'you' were a series of momentary impressions like frames on old-fashioned film. By running the film together we get the impression of a single, walking, talking, thinking person. However, all there *really* is a series of single frames of sensation that create the illusion of 'you'.

More conversation

a) Think back to things you did yesterday, last week, or five minutes ago. Are these things that 'you' did, or are they just momentary impressions and you are being tricked into thinking it is you?

b) Is there any such thing as 'you' or are you just frames of a film?

P.P.S.

Hume also did not believe in laws of nature (eg that water will turn to ice at 0°C). Instead, he believed we just got used to this happening. He said that we see a 'cause' (the temperature goes down to 0°C) and an 'effect' (water turns to ice) and presume that the two are connected. Yet in the grand scheme of the universe there could be something completely different going on.

Even more conversation

a) Imagine you are a dog and every morning you watch your master get up and then the sun comes out. Would it be reasonable to think that your master makes the sun come out? Would you be right?

b) Could there be some hidden cause that links 'cause' (eg dropping a stone) and 'effect' (it falls to the ground)? What could it be? (Make up something fanciful if you like.)

c) If a baby watches a magician make a stone 'rise', how surprised would they be? What does this tell us about getting used to 'laws of nature' we perceive? Are these laws just things we have come to accept instead of things that have been proved?

BIG IDEA 59:
Philosopher 7 — Kant

Note: this discussion will be less thorny if you have already spoken about some of the other philosophers, particularly Hume and Plato.

BACKGROUND BRIEFING

Immanuel Kant (1724–1804) lived a relatively uneventful life around the town in Konigsberg in East Prussia. He was very regular and orderly. Indeed, apparently people in Konisburg used to set their watches by him as he passed by their doors at the same time each day. He was an early believer in democracy and the rights of man. Kant, like philosophers before him, studied how we could use our reason and senses to find out about the world. However, unlike Hume and Locke, he thought that reason, independent of the senses, could also play a role.

Conversation

a) Time and space are two features of the world that are 'beyond' us. They exist whether or not humans exist.

    a. How do we find out about time and space?

    b. What senses do we use to perceive them?

    c. Could our senses only give us a partial picture of time and space?

    d. Can we use our reason to understand more about time and space? Or is reason too tied up with and limited by our senses?

P.S.

Kant wrote about the distinction between 'things in themselves' and 'things as they appear to us'. Things in space and time (eg gravity, tables) for example can have an existence in themselves. However, we learn about these things as they appear to *us*. Space and time filter the perception of these things so that we can only see them through the filter (like putting red cellophane onto our glasses).

Kant thought that our knowledge could not 'transcend' or go further than experience, but we *could* use starting ideas (or 'a priori' ideas) such as 1+1=2 as part of our thinking, even if they did not come from experience. He wrote about this is his most famous work *A Critique of Pure Reason* (1781).

More conversation

a) Is 1+1=2 an 'a priori' idea, or do you think it is based on our experience of counting real things?

b) Could it be that counting real things to get to 1+1=2 is a way of a child *learning* the idea of 1+1=2, but still the *concept* of 1+1=2 does not need real things to count?

c) Can we go further with reason than our senses allow? Can we ask good questions about 'where does space come from' and 'what is the Big Bang' when we can have no sense of them at all? Or are these questions based on our senses as well?

d) Do you think even scientists can get good answers about something that we have no 'sense' of (eg is there a sixth or a seventh dimension of space?)

P.P.S.

Kant also said that there is a moral law that exists. He said that it has the same validity as physical laws. This law is known as the 'categorical imperative'. He also stated that people should be moral because it is their duty, not simply because they want to benefit personally. The categorical imperative is 'Act only according to a maxim by which you can at the same time will that it shall become a general law'.

Even more conversation

a) Do you think that moral laws can be as real/true as laws about gravity and other physical laws?

b) Can you think of a moral law that could be as true as a physical law?

c) Do most people act morally (eg don't steal/attack people) because it is their duty or because they want to benefit personally?

a. Who would the duty be to?

b. What could you get out of a law that says 'don't steal'?

d) The categorical imperative basically means 'act in such a way that if *everyone* did the same, the world would be a good place'. Does this sound like a good base for your actions? Does it sound like other moral guidance you have heard?

e) Kant thinks you should not look at the *effect* of an act to work out whether it is good, just the *principle* of it. So, for example, stealing is bad no matter what the effect of it is. Do you agree with this? Think about:

a. stealing to give to charity

b. lying to an enemy to help your country's troops escape

BIG IDEA 60:
Philosopher 8 — Hegel

BACKGROUND BRIEFING

Georg Hegel was born in 1770, worked as a professor in Berlin in his later life and died in 1831 of cholera. He is best known for his idea of 'the dialectic' — that reason is a process that occurs over time and that there is never really a final 'answer'.

He said that all ideas start with a 'thesis' (eg school discipline should involve terrorising students and beating children) then an 'antithesis' (eg all misbehaving students should be understood and counselled) then a 'synthesis' (eg school behaviour management should involve a blend of non-physical sanctions, such as a detention, combined with discussions with students to get to the base of the problem). Then there would be a new antithesis to challenge the synthesis, and on and on reason would go.

Conversation
a) Can you think of any other ideas where there have been

thesis, antithesis and synthesis? (eg worker's rights).

b) Hegel thought that however good our ideas are now (a synthesis), newer, stronger ideas are going to come and knock them off their perch (ie a new antithesis and synthesis). Does this mean we can never get to the final, right, idea? Does this mean that there is no such thing as a final, right idea?

c) If there is no final, right idea, what is the point of philosophy?

d) Hegel thought there was no 'reason' above human reason. What do you think of this?

e) Hegel thought ideas were not 'right' or 'wrong', but 'right or wrong' for their time. There was no 'timeless' human knowledge.

    a. If someone thought slavery was right 2,000 years ago (ie when almost everyone thought slavery was okay) were they right?

    b. If someone thought slavery was right 150 years ago (ie when a civil war was fought over the issue in the US) were they right for their time?

    c. If someone thinks slavey is right now, could they still be right now?

    d. Can what is 'right' change over time?

f) The dialectic way of thinking allows people with very different views to sit down, talk things out and perhaps come to a way of thinking that combines the best of both of their ideas. How do you think this might work with:

    a. someone who loves owning guns and someone who thinks they should be banned?

    b. someone who thinks social media is great and someone who thinks it has nothing to offer and wastes everyone's time?

P.S.

Hegel believed in a 'world spirit', which was human knowledge and human understanding getting stronger and stronger. Indeed it was like something coming into consciousness of itself. He also thought that human development was, overall, a positive thing. We move towards more freedom, greater rationality, more 'self-development' and more 'self-knowledge'. In this sense Hegel was an optimist about human development. He also said the world spirit 'returns to itself' in three stages: i) in an individual; ii) in the family and society; and iii) in art, religion and philosophy.

More conversation

a) What do you think about a 'world spirit'? Could this be true?

b) Do you agree with Hegel that humanity has improved as time has passed? Do you think we are more rational than we were 500 years ago?

c) By having these sorts of conversations with your parents, are you more 'rational' and 'self-developed' than they were at the same age?

BIG IDEA 61:
Philosopher 9 —
Kierkegaard

BACKGROUND BRIEFING

Soren Kierkegaard was born in 1813 in Copenhagen. His father was well off and his mother was a maid in the household before the two married. Kierkegaard attended the School of Civic Virtue and often wandered the streets of Copenhagen in his youth speaking to all of the maids and manservants. Friends reported that he wore his hair six inches above his head, and this was long before the invention of styling mousse.

He wrote books such as *Either/Or* in which two characters, A and B, had discussions on a range of topics. In his writings he disagreed with the philosophers' project to find 'the truth'. He thought it made more sense to look for individual truths that made sense of each individual life. He died at the age of 42 in 1855 after a fall.

Conversation

a) Do you think there is there a *single* truth for everyone that we should go looking for?

b) Can there be different *truths* between you and your best friend about the following ideas:

  i.   whether your teacher is good?
  ii. why the parents of another friend got divorced and whether it was mainly one partner's fault?
  iii. whether you are sitting on a chair or whether it is just an illusion?
  iv. whether 2+2=4?
  v.   whether you should obey your parents and sleep in your bed tonight, or disobey them and go wandering about the city all night?
  vi. whether you should cheat on a maths test?
  vii. whether Plato or Aristotle is more right about philosophy?
  viii.whether killing people to rob them is bad?
  ix. whether the US is a larger country than Zimbabwe in Africa?
  x.   whether the US is a wealthier country than Zimbabwe?
  xi. whether the US is a better country than Zimbabwe?
  xii. whether there is one truth, or a different set of truths for each person?

c) Can what is true for you about life be false for your best friend? Can you both be right?

d) Can there be a different truth for each individual, that is a 'truth for me' instead of 'the truth'?

P.S.

Kierkegaard said that the most important thing for each person was their own existence, and thus a general description about human nature is not very interesting. He felt that there were objective truths out there such as 2+2=4, but these were not important to each individual's existence either. He felt the most important truths (such as whether someone else loves you) are not available to every person.

a) Do you think that people should try to think about general human nature, or focus on their own existence and what it means to them?

    a. What would be the danger if someone focused mainly on a general idea about humanity being good or bad?

    b. What would be the danger if someone focused only on their own existence to find truth?

b) Can you know if someone else loves you? Or do you just have to trust or believe it?

c) If you do something wrong to someone else and they say they forgive you, can you know that you have been forgiven?

BIG IDEA 62:
Trusting your senses

Note: These ideas are also explored in the philosophers Plato, Aristotle, Locke and Hume.

BACKGROUND BRIEFING

We have five senses; sight, sound, taste, hearing and smell. Through these five channels we sense everything that we know about the world. We take them for granted, and we assume that the information they are giving us is reliable. But is it?

Conversation

a) How do you know that what you see as the colour red is what other people see as the colour red? Could you all be using the same word 'red' to describe different colours?

b) If you were seeing different colours for 'red', how would you ever find out?

c) Are 'colour blind' people really colour blind? Or could

everyone *else* be colour blind?

d) Is 'colour' a real thing at all? Or is it just how humans have evolved to 'see' light waves?

e) Imagine someone who cannot see visible light but can 'see' infrared and X-ray light. Are they blind?

f) Imagine that everyone in the world could 'see' infra-red light except you. Would that make you disabled? Would it make you blind?

g) A car 50 metres away from you looks smaller than a car 5 metres away from you. However, you know they are probably both the same size. What is happening with your eyes and your mind so that you are not confused?

h) Imagine you are crawling through a desert, almost dead with thirst, and you see a mirage of an oasis. What is happening? Have your eyes started to fail, or your mind?

i) Some people love the taste of curry. Other people hate it. However, it is the same taste sitting on genetically similar tongues. How can people perceive it differently? What is happening?

j) Some people love a type of music (eg dance music) while other people hate it. Yet everyone has genetically very similar ears. How can people perceive music differently? What is happening?

k) Imagine that you are walking down a lonely road on the way home when an alien spaceship lands. Aliens get out, tell you the meaning of life then dance in a strange 1970s way using a disco ball from the spaceship. You faint. When you wake up, the aliens are gone. You have forgotten the meaning of life but recall the dancing. Do you believe your senses which tell you that you saw this, or your reason which tells you it is impossible? What do you do?

l)   You have five senses. Can you trust them to give you good information about the world? Could they be deceiving you?

BIG IDEA 63:
Your own superpowers (be careful what you wish for)

a) Imagine that you could fly. What would your life be like? How would the world change for you?

b) Imagine that you could live until the age of 10,000. What would your life be like? How would the world change for you?

c) Imagine that you had the strength of 20 men. What would your life be like? How would the world change for you?

d) Imagine that you could make yourself invisible whenever you wanted. What would your life be like? How would the world change for you?

e) Imagine that you could breathe underwater as well as above ground. What would your life be like? How would the world change for you?

f) Imagine that you could turn yourself into the appearance of anyone else you liked. What would your life be like? How would the world change for you?

g)   Imagine that you (and you alone) could stop time and live in the gaps for up to day at a time. What would your life be like? How would the world change for you?

h)   Imagine that you could learn everything (eg in a book) by downloading it into your head, and that it only takes a few seconds each time. What would your life be like? How would the world change for you?

i)   Imagine you could make anything you touch turn into gold (unless you wore gloves). What would your life be like? How would the world change for you?

j)   Imagine you could make other people turn into a pillar of fire just by looking at them. What would your life be like? How would the world change for you?

k)   Imagine that you could control other people's emotions — you could make people love or hate you, fear you or anything else. What would your life be like? How would the world change for you?

BIG IDEA 64:
All about thoughts (part one)

BACKGROUND BRIEFING

We think about *things* — people, ideas, events — all of the time. But we hardly ever think about thoughts themselves. Yet they are the very things we are thinking *with*. Although it can be dizzying to do this, sometimes it is good to turn the telescope around so that it faces back in — so that instead of looking out at the world, we are looking in at our thoughts.

Many philosophers write about thoughts (see Big Ideas 52–61). However, the conversation below is a lighter, more general conversation. Thinking about our thoughts etc is part of a branch of philosophy called 'The Philosophy of Mind'.

Conversation

a) Where does a thought come from?

b) Where does a thought go when you have finished thinking it?

c) Are you made up of your thoughts? Or are thoughts something that happen to you?

d) Can thoughts 'come to you'? Or do you have to think them?

e) The philosopher Spinoza thought that people may not think, but instead have thoughts 'flow through them'. What do you think of this? Is it persuasive? Could thoughts be alive if they flowed through people?

f) Are your emotions thoughts? Are your emotions made up of thoughts?

g) Is your personality just made up of thoughts?

h) How are your thoughts connected to your brain?

i) If a large cannonball fell on your head and you stopped thinking forever, would you have died, even if your body was still breathing etc?

j) Can a thought be broken up into smaller pieces? Or is a thought the basic unit?

k) Can you have a thought if you had spent your life alone in a dark, soundproof box all your life?

   a. Can you have thoughts if you have nothing to have a thought about?

   b. Could you have a thought about darkness if you had never seen light?

   c. Could you have a thought about yourself if you had never met anyone else?

BIG IDEA 65:
All about thoughts (part two)

a) Do your thoughts make up who you are, or does something else?

b) If you really love someone, are your thoughts in love as well? Can thoughts be in love?

c) If your mother tells you a thought (eg Earth is the third planet from the sun) and then you have it:

    a. is your thought the same as hers?

    b. is it a copy of hers?

    c. is it identical to hers?

    d. what if the thought was 'it's a nice day today' instead?

d) If you have lots of good thoughts, but don't act on them, does this make you a good person?

e) Can thoughts ever be visible?

f) Electro-scanners have pictured electrical activity in the brain when people think.

    a. Does this mean that thoughts are a type of electricity?

    b. Is this *all* thoughts are?

g) Imagine a ride you have been looking forward to for months — the wildest most extreme roller coaster ride. Can your thoughts of this ride be actually better than doing this ride? Think about:

    a. your anticipation in the weeks before

    b. your memories in the weeks after

h) What are the differences between the following types of thinking? Which ones do you like doing the most? Which do you like doing the least?

    a. imagining

    b. wondering

    c. remembering

    d. anticipating

    e. fearing

    f. re-evaluating

i) Think about the thoughts you have in your sleep. Are these different to day time thoughts? Why/why not?

j) Think about the thoughts you have about thinking. Are these different to regular thoughts? Why/why not?

k) Can you think without words? Can a child who is brought up in the woods by mute wolves think?

l) Can dogs think? Can fish? Can oysters?

m) When a computer beats you in chess, is it thinking?

n) Can the most powerful computer in the world think?

o) How could you tell if a computer was thinking for itself?

p) Can you imagine a time in the future where computers can think for themselves?

    a. Would we have then made a new species?

    b. Would we have to look after this new species?

    c. Would this new species dominate us?

q) Do thoughts feel like electricity? What do thoughts feel like (what does electricity feel like?)

r) Just imagine that all of the people and animals in the world suddenly vanish. Are there any thoughts left on the planet?

    a. in books

    b. in computers

    c. in the results of people's thoughts (eg inventions such as cars)

Can there be thoughts at all if there is no-one to think them?

BIG IDEA 66:
Tax

BACKGROUND BRIEFING

Tax is an amount of money that is paid by people (either as individuals or in corporations) to a government. A failure to pay the money can be punished by the government. The government uses the money broadly to provide services for people. These services can include such services as roads, hospitals, schools, sewers, defence, research and social security.

Conversation

a) Should people pay tax? Why/why not?

b) What would happen if everyone stopped paying tax?

c) What would happen if everyone paid twice as much tax?

d) Should you pay tax when you grow up and start earning money?

e) Many people don't like paying tax and try to reduce the amount they have to pay. Why do you think this happens?

Should this happen?

f) Some people avoid paying tax altogether. This is usually against the law. What should happen to these people? Should they go to gaol?

g) If a government spends $1 billion on a road and then charges people $5 each time they drive on it, does this count as a tax? Or is this a charge for using a product?

h) Most countries have a progressive tax rate. This means you might:

    a. pay 10% tax on the first $40,000 you earn,
       pay 20% tax on the next $40,000 you earn,
       pay 30% tax on the next $40,000 you earn and so on.
       Do you agree with this?

    b. Supporters of this approach say that wealthier people should pay more tax because the first $40,000 anyone earns is used to buy vital products such as food and the 400,000th dollar someone earns is used on less vital things for life such as holidays or luxury items. People need the 400,000th dollar less, and thus it should be taxed more. What do you think of this argument? Do you agree with it? Why?

    c. Opponents of this argue for a 'flat tax', for example 20% on every single dollar earned. They say that everyone should pay tax at an equal rate because everyone uses the roads/schools/hospitals etc equally. What do you think of this argument? Do you agree with it?

    d. What do you think the 'top' tax rate should be: 40%, 51%, 90%?

i) England has twice attempted to create a 'poll tax' in which each person pays the same amount of tax once per year. (Once in 1381 and once in 1990. It caused revolts both times.) What do you think about a poll tax compared to progressive income tax?

j)   Many countries have an 'inheritance tax' in which a dead person's assets (eg their house) are taxed before they are transferred to their children or other beneficiaries. Do you think this is a good idea? Why/why not?

P.S.

Robert Nozick (1938–2002) is a libertarian philosopher who holds that the forcible taking of money from people who earned it to give to other people is unacceptable. Indeed, he sees it as similar to a form of slavery — forcing one person to work for another. The slave owner is everyone else in the state who are the partial owners of you.

More conversation

a) What do you think of Robert Nozick's views? Is tax wrong?

b) What do you think would happen to the country you live in if no-one was taxed? Is it a place that you would want to live?

c) Is it acceptable to agree on tax in principle but try to bend or break the rules so that you have to pay as little as possible of it yourself?

Some people try to move their own wealth or their company's operations to countries with much lower rates of tax. Is this acceptable? If it is not acceptable, are there things that governments can do about it?

BIG IDEA 67:
Charity

BACKGROUND BRIEFING

Over a billion people — 20% of the world — live in what the World Bank calls 'extreme poverty'. In 2005 the World Bank defined extreme poverty as those living under $1.25 per day. This is below the level for families to receive basic food and shelter, or allow them to enjoy fundamental rights.

Conversation

a) Should people with money to spare give money to assist those in other parts of the world who are starving? Why/why not?

b) Would it be reasonable to give:

a. money that would otherwise be used to buy shares?

b. money that would otherwise be used to go on a holiday?

c. money that would otherwise be used to go to the movies?

d. money that would otherwise be used to pay the rent?

e. money that would otherwise be used to buy meat and slightly more expensive food for the family?

c) When your family earn money, what things are necessary to buy and what things are surplus? Should you use the surplus money in some other way?

d) Should people with money to spare give money to assist areas such as cancer research in their own country?

e) Does giving money to feed people suffering from extreme poverty make those people *dependent* on handouts? If it means they eat, does it *matter* if it makes them dependent?

P.S.

Onora O'Neill (1941–) wrote about 'Lifeboat Earth'. She compared the Earth to a lifeboat in which a small group of people had all the supplies they needed (and more) to bob gently on the ocean and wait for a rescue vessel to pick them up. However, in doing this the members of the lifeboat ignore someone who is drowning and begging for help just 10 metres away in the water. The captain of the lifeboat states that it's not their fault the other person is drowning, so they have no obligation to do anything about it. Just as Onora O Neill says the actions of the life boat captain are unconscionable, so too are the acts of people in the developed world who fail to make a small effort to save the lives of people in other parts of the world.

More conversation

a) Do you agree with the comparison that Onora O'Neill has drawn between a lifeboat and the world?

b) Do you see flaws in the analogy? If you don't (or if the flaws are not big) does it change your views about income and charity?

c) Do people have a right to do whatever they want with money that they earn? If someone has earned their money fairly, do they have the right to set it on fire in their backyard?

d) Do people have any moral obligation to spend the money that they earn in particular ways?

e) What does your family want to DO as a result of this discussion?

BIG IDEA 68:
Wisdom

a) What is wisdom?

b) Can someone who knows an enormous amount still not be wise? Why?

c) Can someone who has an enormous amount of experience still not be wise? Why?

d) If you had a discussion about each of the questions in this book, would that make you wise? Why/why not?

e) If you change your mind a lot, does that make you more or less wise?

f) Can you become wise through training, or do you need to have a big brain to start with? Can anyone become wise if they try hard enough?

g) If you were to aim to get wisdom in your life what would you do?

P.S.

THE HUMILITY THEORY

In Plato's *Apology* Socrates was said, by the Oracle at Delphi, to be wise. Socrates didn't believe this because he felt that he did not have either a lot of knowledge or wisdom. Socrates then went and interviewed people who stated that they had a lot of knowledge or a lot of wisdom (craftsmen, politicians, poets, law makers etc). In all cases he found that they had a lot less knowledge or wisdom than they claimed to have. Thus, he held, one of the chief features of wisdom is humility and a belief that you did not have all of the answers.

THE KNOWLEDGE THEORY

Versions of this theory are suggested by Aristotle and Descartes. Knowledge is not necessarily deep or expert (you can be an expert in something narrow and still not be wise) but rather knowledge involves an understanding of what is important. Aristotle breaks knowledge down into theoretical wisdom (about scientific truths, logic etc) and practical wisdom (about how to live well).

More conversation

a) If you think you are wise, is that good enough evidence to show that you are not really wise?

b) Which do you think is more important: Aristotle's theoretical wisdom or his practical wisdom?

c) Can young people be wise, or do you need the experience of older people?

d) How important is wisdom in each person? Is it more important for people to be courageous or compassionate than wise? If you could only have two of these three characteristics, which two would you take?

e) How important is wisdom in the world? Could the world get on without people who were wise?

f) How would the world be different if everyone aimed for wisdom instead of material gains?

g) If you were appointed 'Minister for Wisdom' in the government, what would you do to go about trying to get as much wisdom as you could into society?

BIG IDEA 69:
How smart is your pet?

a) How smart is your dog/cat?

b) Do animals such as dogs have their own language? If so, what can they express or say in their own language?

c) If animals had voice-boxes shaped like ours, do you think they would be able to learn our languages?

d) Imagine the sentences 'I hate baths. My owner just got the bath out. I had better go and hide under the sofa'.

    a. Can a dog think this?

    b. Does a dog feel this?

    c. Does it use human words or dog words?

    d. What goes on in a dog's mind as it runs away from a bath and hides under the sofa?

e) Do you think pets can have thoughts? Can they have feelings? Do they have minds?

f) If you teach a pet words such as 'come' 'sit' 'stay' and 'turn around', do they think using these words, or is the action then automatic in a trained dog?

g) If a cat feels 'happy' how similar or different is it to human happiness? What makes it different or similar?

P.S.

Anthropomorphism: This occurs when people assume that animals have human-like qualities on the basis of the animal's actions. However, what people are doing is simply translating what a human would be thinking/feeling if *they* did that action.

Beatrix and Allan Gardner taught chimpanzees to speak using at least 132 American sign language signs and used this to show that chimps could indeed use language. However, this research was criticised by Herbert Terrace who cast doubt on whether these animals were really 'speaking' or simply imitating their trainers.

More conversation

a) Do you think you anthropomorphise your pets? When/How?

b) Do you think your dog/cat *knows* it is a dog or a cat? What happens when you put him/her in front of a mirror? (the scientist Gordon Gallop says that this proves that animals have a concept of themselves).

c) Even if your dog knows it is a dog, do you think they know themselves? Would they recognise themselves in a line-up of three dogs of the same breed?

d) Can animals have beliefs?

e) Could you ever teach an animal to understand whole sentences?

f) Could the smartest animal in the world go to kindergarten?

g) Do you think the following animals can have thoughts at all:

a. whales?

b. dolphins?

c. cats?

d. birds?

e. lizards?

f. fish?

g. mosquitos?

h. oysters?

i. plankton (one-celled sea organisms)?

h) Is there a bigger difference between a dog and a human or a dog and an insect?

i) Are people just another type of animal, or are we completely different? How? Why?

BIG IDEA 70:
Do the right thing

a) You often hear people tell you to 'do the right thing'. How do you *work out* what is the right thing?

b) How important are the following in working out the right thing to do:

    a. your parents?

    b. your religion?

    c. your country?

    d. books?

    e. conversations with people about ethics — trying to think it out for yourself?

    f. your own 'gut' feeling?

    g. anything else?

c) Is there a 'right' thing to do, or is right whatever you choose?

    a. If everyone in your class thought that stealing (eg from each other's pencil cases) was okay, would it be okay?

    b. If almost everyone in the country thought that murder was okay, would it be okay?

d) Are there some acts that are wrong, no matter what almost everyone else thinks?

P.S.

Immanuel Kant was a *deontologist*. He held that some acts (eg lying) were wrong, regardless of their effect on people. He felt that ethics were based on rules and a person's duties to others. His most famous statement is the 'categorical imperative' where he wrote 'Act only according to that maxim whereby you can, at the same time, will that it should become a universal law.' This means when you act, think about what the world would look like if everyone did that act legally. If the world would be a good place if everyone did the act, then go ahead and do it.

Jeremy Bentham (1748–1832) and John Stuart Mill (1806–1873) on the other hand were *utilitarians*. They believed that you judged whether an act was good or not based on its consequences. You should ask whether an act (such as lying) causes more pleasure or pain in the world. If it causes more pleasure then it is morally acceptable, if it causes more pain it is not.

a) Your grandmother knits you a jumper for Christmas that you hate and then asks you what you think of it. You have to decide whether to tell the truth or lie.

- a. What would Kant tell you to do, and why?
- b. What would Mill tell you to do and why?
- c. What would your parents tell you to do, and why?
- d. What should you do and why?

b) Imagine that you have found a safe way to electronically rob $10 million from a bank using your laptop. You can then, with

a hit of the 'return' button send the money to famine relief in Africa. (Note: for some strange reason you can't keep the money — it's either leave it in the bank or send it to Africa). Do you do it? Why?

c) You are an ethical doctor staffing an emergency waiting room. There has been an explosion in the cancer research centre and four eminent scientists have been brought to the waiting room in critical danger. They all need organ transplants to survive and continue their cancer research. Then another man staggers into the waiting room. He is a drug dealer who has been shot. The injury is not life threatening but it turns out that all of his organs are beautifully compatible with the four scientists. You realise that if you hasten the death of the drug dealer, you could probably save the lives of all four cancer research scientists.

   a. Do you do it?
   b. Could you ask someone else to do it?
   c. Would it make a difference if one of the cancer scientists was also your mother or father? Should it make a difference?

BIG IDEA 71:
Dying

a) What would the world look like if no-one died? Would it be better or worse? Why?

b) Some scientists believe that they can find technologies and cures so that people will not need to die in the future. Should they go ahead with their research?

c) If you could decide the perfect age for everyone to live to, what do you think it would be? Why?

d) Why do people die?

e) Is dying fair?

f) If someone's mind and memory has completely gone but their body can still breathe and digest food, has that person 'died'?

g) What do different people think happens to someone after they die?

h) If a person has invented something, or written/filmed something, do they 'live on' in those things?

i) Do people live on in the memories of other people? In what way?

j)   If you could find out, right now, the exact day that you were going to die, would you ask for it? How would it change your life?

k)   Why are many people afraid of death?

l)   Some people have their bodies frozen at the point of death so that they can be 'woken up' again at a future time when advanced technology may be able to bring them back to life. What do you think of this? Would you do it?

m) Is there anything you would die for? A loved one? A political cause?

BIG IDEA 72:
What is real?

a) Are the following things real? What are you using to decide whether it is real or not?

(You could try putting all of these in a hat or a saucepan and drawing them out one by one)

- a. the Mona Lisa
- b. a perfect photocopy of the Mona Lisa
- c. the city you live in
- d. a computer simulation of the city you live in that is used for a game
- e. Monopoly money
- f. Australian currency notes
- g. money in a bank account
- h. 2+2=4
- i. the idea that 'all children have the right to enough food and clean water'
- j. someone's belief that everyone should have access to health care

k. your belief that 'there are fairies at the bottom of my garden'

l. fairies

m. aliens

n. a planet circling another sun that no-one has discovered yet

o. friendship with a close friend

p. friendship with a close friend if you don't actually like them very much

q. the oven in your kitchen

r. the recipes in your kitchen

s. the ingredients of a meal in your kitchen sitting on a bench ready to be made

t. a stuffed panda toy that a young child thinks is really alive

u. Sherlock Holmes

v. Kim Kardashian

w. a picture of Kim Kardashian

x. a picture of Kim Kardashian that has been significantly altered by a computer

y. a toy car two inches long

b) **What makes something real? Is it:**

a. you can touch it?

b. you can think about it?

c. you can use it?

d. it is genuine?

e. you believe it

f. something else?

P.S. (INCLUDING SOME PHILOSOPHICAL WORDS)

Ontology is a philosophical term that is used to describe the study of 'being' and this involves the study of 'what is real'. *Realism* is a philosophy that says that there is an objective reality that exists outside our perception of it. Elements of 'idealism' on the other hand suggest that there are only our perceptions. Bertrand Russell (1872–1970) was a *phenomenologist*. He believed that there were only 'mental events' and that they all came together to produce the sense of a mind.

Much of the study of ontology looks at what elements of reality are *objective*, and what are constructed out of our 'world view'.

BIG IDEA 73:
World views

BACKGROUND BRIEFING

A 'world view' is the way a person (or a group) perceives society and/or the world. It is based on their values, background, beliefs and philosophies. It helps to imagine different people looking out at the world with glasses each tinted different colours. However, some people think that their 'tint' is the *only* way of looking at the world and have difficulty when others think differently.

CHALLENGING This section can be quite difficult. It is hard to take on another world view after having lived in your own for so long.

Conversation

a) What is your own 'world view'? Think up three or four beliefs you hold about society, politics etc. How are each of these views affected by:

    a. your background — the society you were brought up in?

b. your family — what values you got from your parents, brothers and sisters?

c. your religious position?

d. your political position if you have one (Labor/Liberal, Republican/Democrat)?

e. your personality (optimistic/pessimistic, outgoing/introverted etc)?

b) Imagine that you are a young person in a village in Africa whose job is to tend the fields. You would like to go to the dusty village school but can't. Your father has been gone for a year fighting in a civil war. You need to walk a mile a day to get water from a well and you have a bowl of food to eat at the end of the day if you are lucky. It is always possible that there will not be enough food. What might be your opinion about the following matters, and how would your world view shape them:

a. asylum seekers coming by boat to Australia or Mexican people crossing the border to the USA?

b. shopping malls?

c. the way money is distributed in the world?

d. extended members of a family living in different suburbs or cities?

e. swimming costumes?

c) Imagine that you are someone who believes that there are an army of invisible moral elves who live all around us. There are dozens of them in every room. Their job is to punish the wicked and raise up the good through hundreds of small acts every day (eg making the wicked trip and fall, giving the moral people a heads-up in a job interview). This belief colours everything else about the world for you. What are your beliefs about:

a. people who get injured?

b. health insurance?

c. social security?

d. achievement at school?

e. any other political/social issue that is in the media at the moment?

d) You may have a political belief and may already feel sympathy towards the views of one political party. Now think about the people who are convinced another political party is right.

a. What do you think their beliefs are? Why do you think they believe them?

b. What is their world view?

c. Can you find merit in the way that they see the world?

e) Come back to your own beliefs. Do you still believe them? Are your beliefs stronger or better informed now that you have considered the world views of others?

BIG IDEA 74:
Beauty

a. If an alien came down to Earth, where do you think it would go for its holidays? What do you think it would find the most beautiful? What could be different about how it judges a beautiful place?

b. What is more beautiful:

   a. a rainforest or a rubbish tip? Why? Can you think of reasons why a rubbish tip could be more beautiful to someone else?

   b. a very pleasant view of a field, or a very grand view of a mountain? Why?

   c. a grand cathedral or a skyscraper? Why?

   d. a Victorian House or a modern design house? Why?

c. How do you decide what a beautiful piece of music is? Is a piece of classical music such as Pachelbel's Canon beautiful if it is widely regarded as very impressive? What about the track that is number one on iTunes at the moment?

   a. Is music just a matter of individual taste?
   b. If music is a matter of taste, why is there music that almost nobody likes?

d. How do you decide what a beautiful piece of art is? Is a piece of art such as the Mona Lisa beautiful if it is widely regarded as very impressive?

e. Is art just a matter of individual taste?

f. How do humans decide what is beautiful? What are all the different elements that we look at?

P.S.

Plato felt that beauty was to be found reflected from an ideal 'world of forms' and that ideas themselves were very beautiful. He thought that poetry and art distracted people from looking for eternal truths.

David Hume thought that it was up to experts to judge beauty. He said that beauty was an interaction between the object and the mind thinking about it. This means that each person judges beauty subjectively, but we all use a 'natural human sentiment' when judging. Therefore we should go to people who have been trained for definitions of what is beautiful.

In 1896, Santayana (1863–1952) described beauty as pleasure. He said that the pleasure was what happened to us when we viewed or experienced something (eg a mountain). The beauty was more in the pleasure itself, not the object (eg the mountain).

More conversation

a) Do you think that an idea can be as, or more, beautiful than a work of art or a piece of scenery? (as Plato suggests)

b) Can 2+2=4 be beautiful? Can an elegant and difficult mathematical proof be beautiful?

c) Do you think we should defer to experts to decide what is beautiful (as Hume suggests). Or is our opinion as good as anyone's?

d) We often hears the phrase 'I don't know much about art, but I know what I like?' Is this a triumph of subjective experience, is it an uneducated statement, or is it both?

BIG IDEA 75: Beautiful people

a) Are supermodels more physically beautiful than the average person walking in the street? Why?

b) How does the average person decide what is physically beautiful? What are they affected by?

c) Who, or what, decides what is beautiful in our society?

d) Are men and women who spend a lot of time at the gym more physically beautiful as a result?

e) Is there an objective way of being able to describe physical beauty?

f) Is beauty fair? Unfair? Either?

g) Imagine a society where everyone at 18 had to get cosmetic surgery to make them look 'average'. This was so they were not judged in their adult lives on the basis of their beauty or lack of beauty. Would this be fair? Unfair? Why?

h) In some countries weight is considered attractive because it means that the person is wealthy enough to be able to feed themselves. Is this a better way of judging or explaining beauty?

i) If someone gets a lot of surgery to change their face, does the result count as beautiful? How is it different to putting on a beautiful mask?

j) What is meant by 'beauty on the inside'? Is it more important?

k) If someone has a positive, friendly, generous character can this show up in their face? Does this make them more attractive or beautiful? Is the reverse also true?

BIG IDEA 76:
Memories and forgetting

a) What is a memory?

b) How long after something happens does it become a memory to you:

    a. five seconds?

    b. an hour?

    c. a year?

c) Where do memories go in your head?

d) If you forget something, where has the memory gone? What has happened in your brain?

e) If you suddenly remember something (eg a password to an internet site) after trying to remember it for days, where has it been in the meantime? Was it forgotten?

f) If a smell or a glance at something makes someone suddenly remember something they did 20 years ago but hadn't thought about since, where have these memories been? Were *they* forgotten?

g) Is anything ever forgotten, or is it waiting in your brain to be retrieved?

h) Some people have a condition where they are unable to make new memories. Can you describe what life would be like for these people?

i) Some people have 'photographic memories' where they remember everything they see or read. What would life be like for these people? Could there be anything wrong with it?

j) If you read a book and completely forget about it a year later, was reading it a waste of time? Why/why not?

k) Is it more important to experience something or remember it?

l) Some people say they have forgotten everything that they learned at school. Have they really? Does this make school a waste of time for them?

P.S.

Philosophers have generally agreed on different types of long term memory:

- procedural memory — such as knowing how to hammer a nail or play a piano
- semantic memory — which is memory for facts and ideas from the world
- episodic memory — such as recalling last year's Christmas Day, or your first day at school

John Locke (1632–1704) has written about the role of memory in creating a personal identity. Everything else changes over time, but your memories persist and are an important part of making you 'you' from one year to the next. Anne Wilson and Michael Ross (2003) have been very interested in autobiographical memories — memories of your own past. They state that people have a strong idea about the type of person that they are and then they partly adjust their personal memories to fit that sense of themselves. (This is the reverse of the usual notion that your accurate memories tell you what type of person you are.) Indeed, they say that if you change your self-perception, you unconsciously go back and alter your memories to 'fix' this.

More conversation

a) Do your memories help create you, as John Locke would state? If you had all of your memories wiped would you still be you?

b) Do you really change your memories to fit your sense of yourself? Can you think of an example? If you went from thinking you were pretty good at tests to thinking you were pretty bad at tests, what memories of yours could change as a result?

c) Imagine that you forget being lost in the shopping mall as a small child. Your mother or father reminds you of this ten years later and you reconstruct it. Is this a real memory?

d) If someone offered you the chance to 'upload' a whole lot of false memories about going to Disneyland and having a fantastic time, would you take it?

e) Some people create false memories of complete childhood incidents that never happened. Why would they do this? How could it happen?

BIG IDEA 77:
Health care and health insurance

a) Imagine that a person with no money breaks his arms and legs in a fall. It costs money to have him in a hospital. Should someone else (eg the government) pay for his hospital care or should he be left with broken arms and legs? Why?

b) Imagine that someone gets a long-term disease such as cancer. There is 50% chance that it can be cured, but it will cost hundreds of thousands of dollars.

    a. Who should pay for this?

    b. If the person can pay for it, but they will have to sell their house and almost go broke, should they do this? Should someone else (eg the government) pay for them?

    c. If the person *cannot* pay for this, should someone else (eg the government) pay for them?

    d. Is it fair if the person who can pay for it but only if they sell their house has to almost go broke, while someone without money receives payment? Should everyone receive support, or no-one?

c) Imagine that someone gets a rare form of cancer. There is a treatment available but it only works for 10% of people and it costs hundreds of thousands of dollars. Should someone else (eg the government) pay for it?

d) Imagine that it costs half a million dollars to cure a person's cancer. The same amount of money could be used to prevent hundreds of people dying in Africa. What should happen to the money? Why?

e) People can buy insurance that (broadly) covers their medical expenses if they get very sick. If people can at all afford it:

   a. Should they be made to take out insurance by the government?

   b. If they don't take out insurance should anyone else (eg the government) pay for some or all of their medical expenses?

   c. Should their employer take out health insurance for them?

f) Should private companies (who aim to make a profit) be able to offer health insurance? Why/why not?

g) Should governments offer health insurance? Why/why not? Is this their business?

h) Should only 'not for profit' groups offer health insurance? Why/why not?

P.S.

In the US in 2011 58% of people had private health insurance. The remainder of the population either paid for health care costs themselves or relied on government medical aid (such as Medicaid).

This aid was generally restricted to the very poor. In 2010 the government passed a health care Act that made it compulsory for people to get medical insurance. In return, the medical insurance companies had to accept everyone (whereas before they could choose not to insure people if they were sick or too big a risk). This means that almost everyone would be insured.

In Britain there is a National Health Scheme which provides medical care to every person resident in the country. It is not an 'insurance' scheme because everyone is covered.

In Australia everyone is taxed at 1.5% to fund a basic medical service called Medicare. People are also encouraged to take out further private insurance. If they are not in a private health fund by the time they are 31 they are taxed more money. This encourages people to get additional health insurance.

More conversation

a) Do you think that there should be private health insurance, as in the US? Is it more or less sensible to have a National Health Scheme as there is in Britain?

b) Some people feel that taking out health insurance is a choice that people should be allowed to make (or not make). Other people feel that everyone should have to take out health insurance. What do you think?

c) Health care has been a hot political issue in the US for a number of years now. What have people been arguing about? What are the arguments for either side?

BIG IDEA 78: Citizenship

BACKGROUND BRIEFING

A citizen is a member of a state. Citizenship suggests that there is a real relationship between the person and the state. Citizenship involves rights (eg to be secure) and responsibilities (eg to vote). In Ancient Greece, where the concept started, it was almost impossible to become a citizen of a (city) state unless your family already was — slaves and foreigners were excluded from citizenship.

Conversation

a) What duties do you have as a citizen to a state? For example:

   a. Should you be made to pay tax to the state?

   b. Should you have to vote in democratic elections for the leaders of the state?

   c. Should you have to join the army for three years as a young person to help defend the state?

   d. Should you have to occasionally go on a jury to help

decide whether other people are innocent or guilty of crimes?

e. Should you volunteer for charity work?

b) **What rights should you get as part of being a citizen? Do they include:**

a. protection by the law from other people?

b. democracy?

c. the right to use people who are not citizens as servants?

P.S.

Pericles in Ancient Athens said 'We do not say that a man who takes no interest in politics is a man who minds his own business; we say that he has no business here at all.'

In the modern world there are two different conceptions of citizenship. One is the 'liberal individualist' citizen which stresses each person's economic life. It says that people should focus on obeying the law, paying taxes and making a living for themselves. The 'civic republican' type of citizen has a broader meaning and focuses on people's political nature. It expects people to take a role in the democracy and get involved in community concerns.

More conversation

a) Should a citizen be obliged to take an interest in and a view of politics? Why/why not?

b) Does a citizen of a country have any duties at all to the country? Or can they choose to do nothing?

c) What would the world look like if everyone was a 'liberal individualist' citizen? What would the world look like if everyone was a 'civic republican' type of citizen?

d) How important is citizenship to you? How would you feel if you lost your citizenship?

BIG IDEA 79:
Luck

BACKGROUND BRIEFING

Luck and chance are very similar. Chance is the likelihood of a random event occurring (eg dice rolling a particular number). Luck — both good and bad — is something that happens to a person (eg they lose a game because the dice rolled a particular number). Moral luck involves being judged more or less favourably due to events beyond your own control (eg you might be judged less severely if you shot someone and missed compared to if you shot someone and killed them).

Conversation

a) If you are smart, how much of your 'smartness' depends on how hard you work and how much of it depends on whether you were born with 'brains'?

b) If you are good looking/attractive how much of this depends on luck? How much of it depends on your personality or your work?

c) Does the ability and willingness to work hard depend on your luck in being born with this trait, or in having parents who encouraged it?

d) Are we entitled to profit from something (eg a high wage) that depends on your good luck?

e) How much does your position in life depend on your work and how much does it depend on your luck?

f) If you shoot someone and miss are you less morally responsible than if you shoot someone and kill them?

g) Imagine that you trip someone and they fall to the floor and graze their forehead. Your best friend trips someone, they fall to the floor, have a brain haemorrhage and die. Are you less morally responsible than your best friend?

P.S. – LUCK AND PREDESTINATION

The word luck only came into the English language in the sixteenth century. Before that the words English speakers used were linked to 'fate' or 'fortune'. Many religions, in their different ways, see fortune or predestination instead of luck as controlling people's lives, either through Karma and reincarnation (versions of Hinduism and Buddhism) or a God controlling actions as a result of choices made by people (versions of Islam, Judaism and Christianity). More recent studies have linked the appearance of luck with characteristics such as 'optimism'.

More conversation

a) Do you think there is any such thing as good luck or is everything controlled?

b) Are some people 'just lucky'?

c) Do you think happy and optimistic people are more likely to be lucky? Is it just luck that some people are made more happy and optimistic?

BIG IDEA 80:
The global village

BACKGROUND BRIEFING

Imagine that the whole world was a village. Imagine that if all seven billion people in the world were reduced to a village of 100 people, then each person in the village would represent the lives of 70 million people. In this village:

- 84 people would be able to read and write and 16 would not
- 74 people would have a primary school education and 26 would not
- 7 would have a university degree and 93 would not
- 87 would have access to safe drinking water (often from a communal well) and 13 would not
- 52 people would live on more than $2 a day and the other 48 would live on less than $2 a day
- 65 would have improved sanitation and 16 would have no toilets at all
- 77 people would have some sort of shelter and 23 would not

- up to 50 people would be undernourished
- 76 people would have access to electricity and 24 would not (of the 76 most would only use it for a light at night)
- 10 people have 86% of the assets of the village (assets of $10,000 get you into the top third)
- the bottom 50 would share 1% of the world's assets

Conversation

a) Where do you fit in the global village?

b) What do you think about this village?

c) If you were going to design a global village from scratch, what would you make all the different numbers above?

d) How much do your assets in the world depend on luck and how much on good management?

e) How much does where you were born in the world depend on luck?

f) How should our views about luck affect the way we see and act towards people with very poor material standards of living?

BIG IDEA 81:
Elections and voting

BACKGROUND BRIEFING

There is a strong (but not universal) sense that democracy is a preferable way to have a government. However, there are many different ways that voting can work. Here we can look at the various different ways that democratic governments have been elected. We can also think about what may be the best form.

Conversation

a) Australia has compulsory voting. If you do not turn up to vote on election day you are fined. Is this a good idea or should you be allowed to choose whether to vote?

b) Australia has two Houses of Parliament — one makes the legislation and the other reviews it. They are called the House of Representatives and the Senate. Is this a good idea, or should there be just one House?

c) Australia has preferential voting (it is called 'two party preferred'). If there are four parties looking for election and you vote for the party that gets the least votes, then your voting form is picked up again. The vote counters look at who you ranked second and give your vote to them instead. If that party is then knocked out, they pick up your vote again and see who you voted for third. This goes on until there are only two parties left. Is this a good idea, or should it be that if the party you vote for is knocked out, then that is the end of your vote (this is called 'first past the post')?

d) Australia has party-based voting. You vote for a party (eg Labor/Liberal). It is the party who chooses who the leader is, and thus who the Prime Minister is. Is this a good idea or should we be able to vote directly for a Prime Minister/President, as they do in the US?

e) Australia is broken up into 150 electorates — geographical divisions with about 100,000 voters in each. Every electorate sends one person to the Parliament. The party who gets the most people voted in from electorates (more than 75 usually) forms the government.

   a. Is this a good idea, or should we simply count how many people in Australia vote for Labor/Liberal and decide who is the government on the basis of who gets the most votes?

   b. Alternatively, should we have much bigger electorates (say one million voters) who send *ten* people to the Parliament instead of one? This would give smaller parties more say, for better and for worse.

f) Australia elects a new government every three years and then the government makes policy decisions.

   a. Is this a good idea or should voters be allowed to vote

       every few months on whether an individual law should be
       passed (as they did in Ancient Greece)?

b. Is this a good idea or should it be longer (the US has four
       years and Britain has five years)?

BIG IDEA 82: Eradicate It?

BACKGROUND BRIEFING 1 – SOCIAL MEDIA

Social media is people interacting on the internet as they create material, share it, comment on it and revise it. It is often called Web 2.0 and is distinguished from 'traditional' websites which upload content that doesn't change. Facebook, Instagram, Formspring etc are all social media.

Conversation

a) If you could eradicate all traces of social media from the Earth, so that it had never been and never would be, would you do it? Why?

b) How would the world be better or worse without social media?

BACKGROUND BRIEFING 2 – THE INTERNET

The internet began in the late 1960s as a way of connecting computers in academic departments in the USA and was based on an idea by JCR Licklider. The first link between two computers was made in October 1969. The network became open for commerce and other applications in the late 1980s and began being used widely in the 1990s.

Conversation

a) If you could eradicate all traces of the internet from the Earth, so that it had never been and never would be, would you do it? Why?

b) How would the world be better and worse without the internet?

BACKGROUND BRIEFING 3: TELEVISION

The first images were transmitted electronically in 1878 and there were regular breakthroughs in inventions in the 1920s. The British Broadcasting Service began transmitting regular images in 1936 and a television was 'premiered' at the 1939 World Fair. Commercial programmes began to be transmitted in the late 1940s.

Conversation

a) If you could eradicate all traces of television from the Earth so that it had never been and never would be (and nothing like it was ever invented) would you do it? Why?

b) How would the world be better and worse without television?

BACKGROUND BRIEFING 4: FIREARMS

Very basic firearms (ie guns) appear to have been first developed in China in the twelfth century. They came to Europe either through the Silk Road or as part of a Mongol Invasion in the thirteenth century. The nineteenth century saw an 'advance' in the type of guns, with revolvers introduced in the 1830s and rapid fire (or semi-automatic) guns in the 1860s as part of the US Civil War.

Conversation

a) If you could eradicate all traces of firearms from the earth so that they had never been invented and never would be, would you do it? Why?

b) How would the world be better and worse without firearms?

BACKGROUND BRIEFING 5: CARS

The first internal combustion engine to transport a person appeared in 1807 and Carl Benz patented a motorwagon in 1886. In between there were many incremental inventions that went into the creation of the motorcar. Cars were novelties in the late nineteenth century. In the early twentieth century they were popularised by Henry Ford who mass produced a Model T four seater from 1908-1927.

Conversation

a) If you could eradicate all traces of firearms from the Earth so that they had never been invented and never would be, would you do it? Why?

b) How would the world be better and worse without private motorised transport?

P.S.

Choose other inventions. See what the world would look like if it had never been invented. Does the world look better or worse?

If you freeze the world's technological development at a particular point to allow the greatest amount of eventual happiness in the world, where would you freeze it? Now? Twenty years ago? A century ago? Why?

Some big thinkers and what they said

Note: These thinkers are discussed throughout the book and Big Ideas 51–60 in particular focus on what nine giants of philosophy propose.

Aristotle (in the Nicomachean Ethics Book VIII) stated that there are three types of friendship — although you can be friends with one person for several of these reasons.

a) friendships of pleasure, where you get enjoyment yourself out of being the friend

b) friendships of utility, where the friendship is useful to you

c) friendships of virtue, where you are friends because of the person's good character

Anaximanes held that the most basic substance is the world was air/vapour.

Jeremy Bentham was a utilitarian. He believed that you judged whether an act was good or not based on its consequences. You should ask whether an act (such as lying) causes more pleasure or pain in the world. If it causes more pleasure then it is morally acceptable, if it causes more pain it is not.

Harold Bloom, in 'How to Read and Why', said that we should read to help construct, create and make ourselves. He says we read to increase our wit, our imagination and our sense of intimacy. He also said that we read to 'search for a difficult pleasure'.

Nick Bostrom suggested that it is quite probable that we are all living in a simulated reality in some form of gigantic computer.

LEJ Brouwer held that maths itself is something created by human beings, that is, invented. Intuitionists believe that there are no fundamental principles (such as addition) already existing in the world waiting to be discovered.

Democritus held that the basis of all things, including souls, were uncuttable atoms.

René Descartes said that we may all be in the middle of a dream but we know that we exist because we can hear ourselves thinking (I think therefore I am).

Frank Drake devised a calculation that estimated the chance of aliens existing and called it 'The Drake Equation'. It estimated the chance of various occurrences around the universe, such as planets having conditions suitable for life and simple life evolving into complex life.

Carol Dweck wrote about people having 'fixed mindsets' or 'growth mindsets' about their abilities. People with fixed mindsets have a static sense of their own intelligence and are concerned with how smart they look. People with 'growth mindsets' seek to improve and learn from setbacks. They have a fluid sense of their own intelligence/brain as a 'muscle' that can be strengthened.

Empedocles thought that there were four basic substances — earth, air, fire and water. These substances mix and separate in many, many different ways giving the impression of constant change.

Enrico Fermi stated that if aliens did exist, we should already have seen them. This is thus an argument for the non-existence of aliens.

Howard Gardner claimed in 1983 that there was not just one phenomenon called 'intelligence' but instead there were 'multiple intelligences'.

Heraclitus held that everything in the world was in a constant state of flux and nothing ever stayed the same.

David Hume thought that it was up to experts to judge beauty. He said that beauty was an interaction between the object and the mind contemplating it. This meant that each person judges beauty subjectively, but we all use a natural human sentiment when judging. Therefore we should go to people who have been trained and nurtured for definitions of beauty.

Pierre Laplace was a determinist who thought that if you could take a complete physical picture of the world at one moment you could predict the events that would happen in the future.
Robert Kane is a libertarian. He wrote about the existence of free will and that people have 'ultimate responsibility' for their actions.

Immanuel Kant was a deontologist. He held that some acts (eg lying) were wrong, regardless of their effects on people. He felt that ethics were based on rules and a person's duties to others. His most famous statement is the categorical imperative. He wrote 'Act only according to that maxim whereby you can, at the same time, will that it should become a universal law.' This means when you act, think about what the world would look like if everyone did that act legally. If the world would be a good place if everyone did the act, then go ahead and do it.

Edward Lorenz came up with the idea that weather, and many other physical systems, were *chaotic*, that is, not predictable at all. He went on to write a paper called 'Does the Flap of a Butterfly's Wings in Brazil set off a Tornado in Texas'? In this paper he suggested that small differences at the start of something can lead to huge differences later on.

James Lovelock suggested that it is incredibly unlikely that the conditions for life should exist on Earth and also stay that way for so long — we are like a Garden of Eden in a space desert. He said that the Earth itself regulates the environment to keep it so perfect for living creatures. It makes sure all of the pieces of nature work together in one big whole. This means 'we may find ourselves and